THE ENDS

Two Young Lovers' Crimes and the Aftermath

First Edition

ISBN 978-1-7336021-3 -

I0201451

Cover Design and Author Photo by Shay Swetech, WoundUpStudio.com

Editing by Kathleen Berry, KathleenBerry.com

Visit the author's website at DoresaBanning.com.

TABLE OF CONTENTS

1: FAILED ATTEMPT

ends: *intentions or aims; outcomes or results; terminations of existence or deaths*

—Random House Kernerman Webster's College Dictionary

ends: *money; from where one lives or hails*

—Urban Dictionary

<u>1947</u>

<u>Mid-July</u>

Next time, the hitchhiking lovebirds would have to execute better, having botched their first try in Texas. They'd have to ensure their target didn't a) get away and b) survive. Perhaps when they got further west, they'd give it another go, as they desperately needed money.

THE ENDS

The final destination of their cross-country trip was yet to be determined. The purpose, though, clear to both of them, was to "find a new life."[1]

Joseph Leslie Hardy, Jr., age 24, and Lois Hunt, age 22, had set out on their journey on Monday, July 14. Their chosen time to travel boasted hot temperatures throughout the United States that year. However, for the sojourners, the rest of the summer and beyond would become oppressive. And it would be their own doing.

They'd departed from the house in which they'd been residing together, Joseph's mom and dad's residence in Kittery, a small fishing village in Maine. The young couple had taken a few belongings with them, only what they could carry comfortably on foot and a small amount of money.

Since they'd left, the two had been "tired, cold and hungry," according to Lois.[2] Some strangers along the way had given them food, and for sleep, they'd resorted to lying in a pasture or random truck bed. Joseph and Lois each had wired and phoned their respective parents, asking for funds, to no avail.

Nine days later, on Wednesday, July 23, the couple arrived

---

1   Reynolds, Ruth, *The Post-Standard*, "Justice Topsy-Turvy When Confusion Confounds Confessions," March 19, 1950.
2   *The Union*, "Hardy Trial Nears Finale," Feb. 1, 1949.

in the Northern California waterfront city of Vallejo,[3] where Lois' only brother Raymond Strong Hunt, 24 and two years older, lived. He'd enlisted in the U.S. Army in 1941, was a World War II veteran and now worked at the Benicia Arsenal, the primary West Coast ordnance facility for that service branch.

Lois and Joseph stayed near Raymond at a nearby rooming house for three nights. The next morning, they borrowed $100 (about $1,150 today) from him and took a bus to Reno to "double our money,"[4] Joseph later would write, by betting it on casino games there. The Biggest Little City was Nevada and the country's legal gambling mecca at the time.

Instead, the duo lost all but a few dollars of their only cash and still lacked an income source. They mailed a thank you card to Raymond and a similar note to Lois' mother, Julia G. Heavilin, in Manitowoc, Wisconsin. Raymond's read:

"This may come as something of a surprise to you but I'm sure you'll understand. We have decided that we do not desire to become a burden to you and so we are leaving. We are very grateful for your assistance and we love you very much. I do hope you will understand and not hate us too much. Goodbye for the last time. Thank you again. Lois and Joey"[5]

---

3   The city was named after General Mariano Guadalupe Vallejo, who'd championed statehood for California.

4   Joseph Hardy and Lois Hunt's written account from the Nevada County Jail, California, 1947.

5   *The Sacramento Bee*, "Brother in Vallejo Will Aid Lois Hardy," Aug. 7, 1947.

On Sunday, July 27, the weary travelers left Reno for Salt Lake City, Utah, founded in 1845 by Mormon pioneers led by Brigham Young. Though Lois and Joseph weren't of their faith, perhaps they'd find an opportunity or build a foundation for a future there.

2: SUSPICIOUS BEHAVIOR

<u>July 31, Thursday</u>

Joshua trees, looking like free-form scarecrows with spiny limbs, punctuated the landscape showcasing various types of brush — sage, salt black and rabbit, to name a few. With the Mojave Desert's rugged flora in their peripheral vision, a pair of rangers patrolled Nevada's Boulder Highway, a 15-mile stretch between Las Vegas and Boulder City.

Las Vegas was in its infancy, but Boulder City was far more advanced. It was the community developed 16 years earlier for the men who were building Boulder Dam and their families.

Mid-morning, the rangers spotted a rolled over 1947 Ford sedan on the side of the thoroughfare, near the small community of Whitney. They stopped to assist.

At the crash site, they encountered a 20-something woman in the car, alone and with an injured shoulder. She said her name was Lois. She was petite and thin. Shoulder-length, naturally wavy, blonde hair framed her heart-shaped face, noteworthy for a high forehead, deeply set blue eyes, downward pointing nose and long chin.

She frantically explained that she and her male companion Joey were on the way to Kingman, Arizona from Las Vegas. She didn't reveal, though, that once there, they planned to abandon the car and catch a bus heading eastward. She relayed that Joey had gone to get help and was walking back the way they just had come.

The men extricated Lois from the mangled metal and put her in their vehicle. While driving toward Boulder City, the trio spotted Joseph, a lanky man with a long neck and limbs, staggering along the shoulder.

They caught up to him and pulled over. Up close, his clean-shaven, chiseled face featured high cheekbones, an angled nose, sharp jaw and narrow chin. His hair was closely cropped with longer bangs swept to one side of his wide forehead. Most noticeable were his piercing, almond-shaped eyes. He was of medium height, slender and close in age to Lois.

Upon the authorities' request, neither Joseph nor Lois produced a driver's license or car registration. When they were asked who owned the car and how they'd come by it, the two faltered and gave vague responses.

The rangers transported the lovers to the Clark County Jail in

Las Vegas[1] for further questioning. Lois, however, first received medical care at the local Clark County Indigent Hospital for what seemed to be a strained or fractured shoulder.

At the lockup, Clark County Sheriff Glen Jones asked the couple who owned the Ford, and Joseph claimed he did. He said he just had bought it in Reno with money he'd won from gambling there. As for why he didn't have documentation of the sale, he said he'd forgotten to get any due to his excitement about his newly acquired cash and his eagerness to leave town with it.

The available evidence, however, contradicted Joseph's statements. For one, Joseph and Lois only had $10 (about $115 today) between them. Two, papers in the car had another man's name on them, which the couple couldn't explain.

"The sheriff ordered the pair locked up until they could give an account of themselves without conflicting detail."[2]

Joseph and Lois were arrested for grand theft auto and detained for investigation. What would come to light would be appalling.

---

1   Nevada's Las Vegas is located in Clark County.
2   *The Sacramento Bee*, "Bridal Couple Lure Man to Death in Hills," Aug. 4, 1947.

3: COMING CLEAN

August 3, Sunday

While still behind bars three days later, Lois Hunt attended a Sunday revival in the jail, conducted by Reverend R. Craig Willoughby, pastor of the Full Gospel Tabernacle.

About halfway through the service, Lois started bawling and blurted loudly, "I want to make my peace. I've got something to confess, but I won't do it without Joey."[1]

Joseph Hardy was retrieved from his cell to join Lois and Willoughby.

"You've got to talk, Joey," she urged. "I've given myself to the Lord, and you must, too."

Joseph remained silent. A beat passed.

"Please, Joey," she pleaded.

---

1   *Nevada State Journal*, "Killers Tell Sordid Story," Aug. 5, 1947.

THE ENDS

"Last Wednesday, I killed a man," he said.

Willoughby called and informed Clark County Sheriff Glen Jones about the couple's revelation. It had to have shocked everyone familiar with their case as they suspected the two of auto theft, a misdemeanor, not felony homicide.

The couple, soon after, found themselves in Jones' office, relaying the recent events to Sheriff's Deputies W.E. "Butch" Leypoldt and Alexander H. Kennedy, who subsequently interrogated them thoroughly. A stenographer recorded their dialogue.

The inmates also memorialized their statements on paper, however, Joseph handwrote them both despite Lois being literate. She supposedly dictated hers to him in the first person.

Joseph signed one of them, which was about two pages long, double spaced. On the other, he wrote, "Witnessed by Joseph L. Hardy, Jr.," and signed his name. Lois signed it, too.

From their confessions, grisly details emerged.

4: HEINOUS ACTS

<u>July 28, Monday</u>

Nearly a week earlier, a Southern Californian bachelor, James William McLain, age 48, was exploring the western U.S., alone, by car. He was three days into a vacation from his job as an elevator operator at the Veterans Administration Hospital in Van Nuys, a Los Angeles city and baseball Hall of Famer Don Drysdale's hometown.

James telephoned his sister Nola to tell her he'd depart Salt Lake City the next morning and drive directly to her and her husband Robert's home in Bakersfield for a visit, en route back to his residence in Burbank, both cities in the state's southern region.

Presumably, to get to the Marlatt residence, James planned to take U.S. Route 40 to Sacramento, also in The Golden State, then travel southward along State Route 99 to the agricultural city.

THE ENDS

<u>July 29, Tuesday</u>

After leaving The Beehive State's capital, blue-eyed, gray-haired, fair-skinned and heavyset James encountered Joseph Hardy and Lois Hunt thumbing a ride just past the state line, where suddenly people could gamble and be served alcoholic drinks, both legally.

He picked them up, perhaps for company and/or to be helpful.

The East Coasters had gotten stranded in Nevada's hot, dry, high desert, when their last ride had refused to take them into Utah. With no facilities in sight, and after having hung out for several hours on the barren land but for scrub brush, "we finally became extremely tired, hungry and thirsty," Joseph would write later.[1] "So we decided to hold up the first car which stopped for us."

It was a Ford. It was James'.

"We forgot our intentions when the driver of the vehicle offered us food and shelter at Sparks, Nevada," Joseph would add.[2]

James drove Lois and Joseph about 515 miles in all, a trip that offered little in terms of other cars on the road and major cities along the way.

The route, which paralleled the Humboldt River, traversed the sagebrush steppe of The Silver State, characterized by a

---

1   Joseph Hardy and Lois Hunt's written account from the Nevada County Jail, California, 1947.
2   Ibid.

preponderance of, well, sagebrush, with its vibrant mustard yellow and white flowers, and perennial grasses.

The occasional mining towns the three passed through broke up the monotonous scenery. Some were mere ghosts of the past. Others, like Elko, Winnemucca and Battle Mountain, were populated and astir.

After about eight hours together on the road, the travelers arrived and stopped in Sparks, a bedroom city to Reno, Nevada's largest metropolis at the time.

James had planned to stay the night there in a cabin, which he'd reserved. He reiterated to the couple his offer to let them crash with him at least until the morning. They accepted.

July 30, Wednesday

Joseph, Lois and James went to breakfast at a Reno restaurant. Then they explored a few casinos to see what they were like but didn't gamble or drink alcohol.

All of the city's gaming establishments were clustered within a few blocks' radius. They encompassed large, popular casinos, such as Harolds Club, the Bank Club, the Palace Club and Harrah's, and numerous smaller houses and saloons.

After, the couple persuaded James to join them on an excursion to the mountains, the Sierra Nevada in California in this case, supposedly on the promise that if he went, he could have sex with Lois. She flirted and led James on to ensure he'd go.

In James' Ford, the trio headed west, crossed the Nevada

13

border into the land of the poppy, redwood and grizzly bear and stopped at a park. Because the spot was public and well trafficked, Lois again used her wiles to convince James to accompany her and Joseph elsewhere.

After traveling further west on Highway 40, they exited it at Hirschdale Road at about 1:30 or 2 p.m., drove about one-eighth of a mile and pulled over.

It was a quiet, woody spot near the remote community of Hirschdale, developed in 1926 as a road stop in the Tahoe National Forest, elevation 5,446 feet. The closest town of any size was Truckee, 13 miles away and home to about 1,350 residents.

The air was crisp and tinged with an aroma of pine. Lois and James walked ahead on a dirt trail. Joseph waited a bit then followed.

At a clearing about a quarter-mile into the Ponderosas, Jeffreys, incense cedars and firs, Lois or James put a small blue pad or mattress on the ground and spread a woven, red plaid blanket over it.

Lois and James embraced. They sat on the makeshift bed. They kissed and caressed one another.

Joseph advanced toward the unfolding scene, stopped close by and hovered. Soon, Lois signaled him with a nod.

When the next train roared by on the nearby Transcontinental Railroad, Joseph fired a 0.32-caliber pistol at James.

James collapsed. Lois retreated.

Now on his back, James gurgled. Lois told Joseph she couldn't stand the noises and blood coming from James' mouth. To remedy both, she coiled Joseph's handkerchief around the end of a stick and shoved it between and past James' lips.

Joseph shot James again ... and again ... in the head.

Lois checked James for a pulse, and he had one!

Joseph scouted out a large rock and with it, bludgeoned James in the head, pulverizing his skull with a coup de grâce blow.

Joseph then dragged James' 5-foot, 8-inch-long body about three yards away to remove him from the sightline of cars on the freeway. The shooter tooktwo watches, car keys and a wallet from James' person then rolled up the blanket with the deceased in it.

The co-conspirators drove away in their victim's Ford, abandoning his lifeless body in that isolated locale.

This individual, James William McLain, who'd offered and provided the destitute couple a lift and a place to stay, was a veteran, though his service had been brief.

As required, he'd registered for the World War I draft in 1918 at age 19. Called to duty, he'd enlisted in the U.S. Army on November 10, 1918, the day before the war had ended with the signing of an armistice. The Army had discharged James three days later, on November 14.

Before living and working in Burbank, for many years James had been a yardman at S.P. Oil Company in Taft, California, the same town in which he and his sister Nola, eight years younger, had spent most of their childhood. He also had lived elsewhere in the state, in San Diego, for a while, where he'd worked at Consolidated Air Craft Corporation.

James had been born in Jackson, Mississippi on June 15, 1899 to George Phillip and Sarah Emma (née Eastwood) McLain.

After committing the murder and robbery, Joseph and Lois stopped at the closest service station, in Hirschdale, where he ordered and drank a whiskey and she, a crème de mente. They then continued westward to Truckee, where they imbibed more alcoholic drinks at a bar. Their next stop was the Sparks cabin to retrieve their luggage.

They drove back to Reno, where they spent the rest of the day and evening playing games of chance and drinking to the point of intoxication, possibly beyond, paying for it all with James' money — $20 in cash and $200 in Bank of America travelers cheques (a total value of about $2,500 today).

Many hours later and hungover, the love-struck criminals set off for Las Vegas, then a city less developed and populated than Reno, its northern counterpart, but on the brink of burgeoning.[3]

The roughly eight-hour drive in James' Ford took them down U.S. Route 95, through mostly uninhabited desert. Joseph

---

3   Las Vegas' population was 8,422 in 1940 and 21,317 in 1950 versus Reno's of 24,624 and 32,497, respectively.

sped, maintaining 85 miles per hour when possible.

Along the way, the couple stopped several times to buy food and drinks and play slot machines. By the time they arrived at their destination, their winnings had increased to $80 ($925 today), they'd say later.

In Sin City, Lois and Joseph would continue what appeared to be celebrating.

18

5: BOUND BY HOMICIDE

<u>July 31, Thursday</u>

Joseph Hardy and Lois Hunt married one another in a quickie chapel ceremony in Las Vegas at about 7:30 a.m., after obtaining the requisite license.

They punctuated the formalization of their union by imbibing champagne and whiskey at the El Rancho hotel-casino on the Las Vegas Strip, a segment of Las Vegas Boulevard heavily concentrated with hotel-casino resorts. Still, the money of deceased James McLain covered all of their expenses.

To Lois and Joseph, their wedding most likely symbolized their devotion to and everlasting love for another. To society, however, it signified the two becoming bigamists, as each already was married to someone else. One wonders if, at the time, Joseph and Lois knew about each other's existing spouse.

Joseph remained betrothed to Virginia Baptiste, a Women's

Army Corps[1] member, and had been since their nuptials on Sept. 20, 1945, held in the chapel at the Camp Croft military base in South Carolina.

Lois really was Mrs. Corliss, wife of Arthur G., a farmer and factory worker. The two had tied the knot on March 22, 1946 and had lived under the same roof in Maine until June 21, 1947, at which time Lois had moved in with Joseph and his parents in Kittery.

Arthur had been Lois' second husband. Her first had been Walter Peret, a mechanic, whom she'd married in Connecticut in 1942. The Perets had divorced three or four years later.

Joseph and Lois discussed their next steps. Maybe they'd go to Texas, perhaps Florida. They hadn't decided on a final destination, only that they should leave the west.

With him at the wheel and her riding shotgun, the "newlyweds" got on the Boulder Highway in Las Vegas, intending to take it all of the way into Northern Arizona. Once there, they planned to abandon James' car and catch a bus to continue moving east.

Shortly, though, due to drunkenness and/or fatigue, Joseph lost control of the vehicle. It toppled and slid to a stop on the side of the road. Lois sustained a shoulder injury in the crash, and she and Joseph were shaken up.

---

1   The Women's Army Corps, or WAC, had been created in January 1944. Its members were assigned to roles previously occupied by men — administrative and clerical workers, hospital nurse's aides and others — so the latter could be used overseas.

He took off on foot toward Boulder City to get assistance. She tossed out the window all documents bearing James McLain's name, including the remaining $60 in travelers cheques.

Over the previous two days, Lois and Joseph had spent $160 (about $1,800 today), more than three-quarters of James' currency they'd purloined.

The rest of the honeymoon phase for "Mr. and Mrs. Joseph L. Hardy, Jr." wouldn't be joyous.

6: WILLFUL, PREMEDITATED MURDER

August 3, Sunday

When Joseph Hardy documented his confession in writing in Las Vegas, he'd explained:

"We started to hitch-hike back to Reno, Nevada ... We were given a ride by a Mr. J.W. McLain of Burbank, California. ...

"He talked too much and gave us the impression that he was just a rich bachlor [sic], and could be taken over very easily. His actions to-ward [sic] Miss Hunt were very vulgar, lewd, and improper, but this only convinced us that he could be easily lead [sic] on.

"Mr. McLain invited us to share a cabin with him at Sparks, Nevada, and we accepted. We stayed there over-night [sic], and he, McLain, tried several times to get Lois to submit to him, which she would not consent to.

"Next morning we had breakfast at a café in Reno, Nevada and at our insistance [sic] started for a trip into the mountains.

23

THE ENDS

We stopped at one state park with the intentions of robbing and killing him, but it was too public, so at Lois' request and promise of her body, Mr. McLain consented to go to a more desolate spot, five miles further into California.

"Mr. McLain wanted to stay in the car, but promised to walk back into the woods if Miss Hunt, now Mrs. Hardy, would submit to his desires. This being ideal for our plan, we consented.

"We all three walked back into the woods about one-quarter of a mile where Mr. McLain took Lois into his arms.

"I remained in the rear about a couple of feet because I was trying to make up my mind to shoot him, but I became nervous and would have backed out had not Lois encouraged me to carry out our plan.

"Lois and McLain seated themselves on a blanket we had brought, and began kissing. Lois turned his head so that he could not see the gun.

"I then shot him through the left ear and he fell back on the ground. Lois moved away from him and I could see that he was not dead, so I shot him two more times. He was still breathing strongly when Lois took his pulse, so I hit him in the head with a large rock. He was dead anyway then.

"I then removed all of his personal property. His two watches, wallet, and car keys is all he had on him."[1]

---

1   Joseph Hardy, Jr.'s written confession in Clark County, Nevada, Aug. 3, 1947.

A note referencing Lois and Joseph and found in his pocket read: "Our score in murder: successful three, Chicago one, California one, Louisiana one. Failed, Missouri, one. We have no regrets except that we have only two corpses to our credit. There are several people who are on our list."[2]

Following the partners in crime's jailhouse confessions, William "Bill" Gautsche, Harold B. Fowler and four other California Highway Patrol (CHP) officers went looking for James in the area the lovers had described.

At around 7 or 8 p.m., the search team discovered James' lifeless, bloated, odiferous and clothed body and noticed two holes in his head. By then, four days had passed since the young couple had abandoned deceased James there, defenseless against the elements and the area's wildlife.

Norval "Tom" F. Dolley, the tall, husky, constable for the town of Truckee, then investigated the crime scene and had it photographed. From it, he collected two bullet cartridges, a stone covered in dried blood and a stick wrapped with a blood-stained handkerchief. He transported James' body to the Truckee Mortuary.

<u>August 4, Monday</u>

H. Ward Sheldon charged that Joseph and Lois "did willfully, unlawfully, feloniously and with malice aforethought, murder one James W. McLain, a human being; all of which is contrary to the statute in such cases made and provided

---

2   *The Sacramento Bee*, "'Innocent' Blonde Bride Tells of Truckee Slaying," Aug. 4, 1971.

and against the peace and dignity of the People of the State of California," according to the information, or document detailing the charge or charges filed against a suspect.[3]

Sheldon was the district attorney of Nevada County, California,[4] the jurisdiction in which Joseph and Lois had slain and robbed James.

The detainees were to be extradited to Truckee from Las Vegas as soon as possible, but it would take a day for the related paperwork to be completed.

In the meantime, they talked freely to reporters.

"This is a heck of a way to spend a honeymoon," Lois said, referring to her and Joseph both being behind bars.[5]

Joseph expressed confidence Lois would be released from jail that day because, in his opinion, law enforcement officials lacked any proof she'd committed a crime.

"My husband and I thought they couldn't keep me more than 72 hours," Lois said. "If I got out, I was going to do a very wicked thing; I was going to get some arsenic. We were both going to commit suicide."[6]

When asked about the two other murders he'd referenced

---

3   Information, *The People of the State of California vs. Joseph Leslie Hardy, Jr. and Lois Hunt Hardy*, Case 8856.
4   Unlike the name suggests, Nevada County is located in Northern California (not Nevada). In 1947, its primary communities were, from the most to least populated, Grass Valley, Nevada City and Truckee.
5   *Berkeley Daily Gazette*, "Newlyweds in State to Face Killing Charge," Aug. 5, 1947.
6   Lois Hunt's interview in Nevada City, California, Sept. 7, 1947.

in a written note, Joseph admitted they'd been hyperbole intended to "glamorize" him and Lois.[7] Perhaps they'd sought to become the Bonnie Parker and Clyde Barrow of the 1940s, glorified outlaws and lovers renowned for their criminal exploits in tandem.

"I wanted to look more of a hero. Just one killing made me look like a sissy," Joseph said.

That night, he and Lois met with Clark County District Attorney Robert E. Jones for what turned out to be "one of the weirdest legal conferences on record," Jones said.[8] During the exchange, Lois sat on Joseph's lap, rocking back and forth, fondling him and nuzzling his neck.

When she wasn't talking, she hummed *The Prisoner's Song,*[9] as if to publicly declare that its lyrics encapsulated her and her Joey's mindset, that if their incarceration continued, they'd pine over one another and their separation.

Oh, I wish I had someone to love me

Someone to call me their own

Oh, I wish I had someone to live with

'Cause I'm tired of livin' alone

Oh, please meet me tonight in the moonlight

7   *Los Angeles Times*, "Psalm Singing Leads to Murder Confession," Aug. 5, 1947.
8   *Nevada State Journal*, "Honeymooning Killers Held in Truckee," Aug. 6, 1947.
9   Written by Guy Massey and first recorded in 1924 by his cousin Vernon Dalhart, this song had been the first in the country genre to sell 1 million records.

THE ENDS

Please meet me tonight all alone
For I have a sad story to tell you
It's a story that's never been told

I'll be carried to the new jail tomorrow
Leaving my poor darling all alone
With the cold prison bars all around me
And my head on a pillow of stone

Now I have a grand ship on the ocean
All mounted with silver and gold
And before my poor darlin' would suffer
Oh, that ship would be anchored and sold

Now if I had wings like an angel
Over these prison walls I would fly
And I'd fly to the arms of my poor darlin'
And there I'd be willing to die

Joseph and Lois recapped to Jones their crimes but cited a different motive this time, one which transferred blame for their unlawfulness from themselves to the victim.

Originally, they'd said they'd killed James to rob him,

28

believing he was wealthy. Now, they claimed they'd murdered him solely because he'd "made passes at" and "tried to take advantage of" Lois. Joseph said he'd told the first version, a lie, to "get right with God."[10]

August 5, Tuesday

Nevada County Sheriff Richard W. Hoskins and Coroner Alvah Hooper transported Lois and Joseph, who'd waived an extradition hearing, the roughly 500 miles to the Truckee Jail[11] in Northern California from the Clark County Jail in Southern Nevada.

En route, the officials stopped with the couple at Walker Lake to search for the gun that Joseph had confessed to having disposed of there. They didn't find it.

Soon after, however, the murder weapon's true location would come to light, and ballistics testing would confirm the cartridges found at the crime scene matched that exact pistol. A Clark County Jail trustee[12] would report that he discovered it in a bag of trash Joseph had handed him, while imprisoned there, immediately prior to a facility-wide check for weapons.

Contrary to his claim, Joseph hadn't tossed the gun in any body of water. Rather, he and Lois had had it in their possession at

---

10   *Nevada State Journal*, "Honeymooning Killers Held in Truckee," Aug. 6, 1947.
11   The Truckee Jail housed inmates from 1875 until May 1964, including some infamous ones, the likes of George "Baby Face" Nelson, George "Machine Gun Kelly" Barnes and, the first woman the state of California executed, Evelita "The Duchess" Spinelli. Today, the building is the Old Jail Museum, open for tours during the summer.
12   A jail trustee was an inmate afforded some responsibility in the running of the facility. Typically, he/she wasn't a serious offender and behaved well during incarceration.

the time of the car accident on the Boulder Highway and the subsequent ride with the rangers to the jail.

When they'd been booked, Lois had snuck it into the building, hidden under her clothes. (She hadn't been frisked at the time because no female officer had been on duty to do it.)

At some point during the newlyweds' four-plus days as Nevada inmates, Lois had handed the firearm off to Joseph, who'd kept it in his cell until the threat of another search had forced him to part with it.

Joseph claimed he'd purchased the gun from a soldier in the men's restroom at the Vallejo bus station, the reason for which is unknown. Later, he'd deny he'd obtained the weapon to kill someone.

"Our plans did not include murder but only a hold-up now and then," he'd write.[13]

Near the end of the extradition trip, Joseph or Lois — the coroner and sheriff would disagree in the future as to whom it'd been — pointed to a spot off of Interstate 80 as they passed it and noted they first had chosen to murder James there but had decided against it when they saw how public it was.

Finally, they all arrived at their final destination. Located in the Meadow Lake township, the Truckee Jail was a two-story, stone and brick building. It contained six individual cells, three on the bottom level for men, three on the top for women,

---

13   Joseph Hardy and Lois Hunt's written account from the Nevada County Jail, California, 1947.

and two larger holding areas.

Because of its smaller size, the jailhouse primarily served as a temporarily place to hold arrestees before they were transferred to the larger Nevada County Jail, in California's Nevada City.

Joseph told Hoskins, "I know this is the end for me but I'm not sorry. I would do it again just as quickly. I didn't like McLain's attitude toward Lois and he had it coming."[14]

Lois echoed Joseph's sentiments, saying, "I'm not sorry. I don't know just how to explain it but I know I'm not sorry. It's just that I can't find the right words to say how I feel. Of course, it was not pleasant, but I have no regrets."[15]

Hoskins placed Joseph in a ground floor cell and confined Lois in an upstairs one, each about 80 square feet in size.

A cute, young, brunette woman named Gladys Dolley appeared at Lois' cell and struck up a conversation with the murderess, who confided in her.

This interaction would affect Lois adversely in the future.

---

14   *The Sacramento Bee*, "Truckee Hearing is Held for 'Kiss of Death' Slayers," Aug. 6, 1947.

15   Ibid.

7: PREVIOUS RAP SHEET

August 6, Wednesday

A will that Joseph Hardy and Lois Hunt prepared while in the Truckee Jail surfaced. They bequeathed all of their belongings — two rings, a gold locket, men's watch, cigarette lighter and $82.49 (mysteriously increased from $10 in Vegas) — to Raymond Hunt.

Hours before Lois and Joseph's first court appearance in Truckee, the couple spoke to the press about their potential fate.

"It would be heavenly to die in the gas chamber with Joey," Lois told reporters.[1]

Her "husband" said, "I know this is the end. I know what's going to happen to me, but I don't care." He gave the newsmen a copy of the letter he'd written days earlier, on August 2, to

---

1   *Portland Press Herald*, "Hardy, Bride Feel Sure of Execution," Aug. 6, 1947.

his mother, Elizabeth A. Hardy (née Novell). It read:

"Dear Mother,

"As this will be my final letter to you ever, I need not pull any punches. Lois and I are in Las Vegas County [sic] Jail on suspicion of murder. We have not confessed yet but plan to today. Yes, Mom, I really killed a man for his money and car. Lois lured him into the woods by her feminine charm and was actually kissing him when I shot him thru [sic] the head. He was stubborn and I had to put three bullets into his head before he died.

"He had a 1947 V8 deluxe car and over $200 in travelers checks so Lois and I went to Reno and had a hell of a good time. Then we went to Las Vegas and got married. We bought some champagne and scotch whisky and got drunk as hell. We started for Texas but I fell asleep at the wheel and we ran off the road and knocking down a telephone pole we rolled over three times. We were not even hurt very much. ...

"Lois and I have decided to end it all so are confessing everything today. It was a lot of fun while it lasted but it was too short. I've tried a thousand times to get Lois to let me take the whole blame but she won't so I guess we'll die together. That's how she wants it.

"Mom, don't let anyone ever tell you that it takes guts to kill someone. I felt no more conscience when I shot him than I would killing a wild rabbit and it has never bothered me since.

"Dad always said I'd die by hanging, but he was wrong; in

California they put you in a gas chamber!!!!

"Well, so long Mom, I guess you'll never miss me much but at least think of me occasionally.

"If the above sounds too heartless or cruel it's only because I'm telling you how it actually happened.

"Bobby [Joseph's younger brother] needn't know of this I guess. Lois sends her love. So long Buddy.

"Jr."

Joseph's childhood had been tainted by some critical factors that may have contributed to his run-ins with the law as a young man. He said of himself that he'd "never lived an honest day"[2] and had "been in trouble in all my life."[3]

Born in Exeter, New Hampshire on April 9, 1923, Joseph had been his "poor but honest" parents' firstborn of five children.

His namesake and father Joseph L. Hardy, Sr. and his mother had been married eight months earlier. Sr. had been 30, and it had been his second marriage. Elizabeth had been 18.

Joseph, Sr. had been employed consistently throughout Jr.'s childhood, at the Continental Shoe Factory in Portsmouth, New Hampshire, and still was at the time of the murder. He may have been an alcoholic, as the local newspaper contained a handful of reports of him having been in car accidents over the years.

---

2   *Long Beach Independent*, "Couple Lures Man to 'Kiss of Death,'" Aug. 5, 1947.

3   *The Des Moines Register*, "Wife, Who Lured Victim, and Slayer in Suicide Pact," Aug. 4, 1947.

Jr.'s mother had been a homemaker. According to the 1940 U.S. Census, a housekeeper and her husband had been living with the Hardys.

The young Joseph had two surviving brothers, Roger L., younger by 10 years (born 1932), and Robert E., 14 years his junior (born 1936). His brother David Andrew had passed away at seven months old in 1939, and another brother, Norman Jean, had died during or soon after birth in 1940.

When Joseph, Jr. had been six years old, the family had relocated from Portsmouth to Kittery, each sited on either side of the New Hampshire-Maine border, respectively. The move took them from a city of about 17,000 residents to a smaller village of about 7,000.[4]

In Kittery, Joseph, Jr. had "gone missing" at age 10 but supposedly had been back at home that night.[5] Had he run away or wandered off and gotten lost?

At age 12, the court had mandated that he attend a local reformatory for juvenile offenders because of his truancy. Accordingly, he went to live and continue his education at the co-ed State Industrial School, in Manchester, New Hampshire.

"Upon my return home, I was bluntly told that I was not welcome and could shift for myself," he said. "However, I remained at home and continued school."

The pattern, Joseph committing a crime, getting sent to reform

---

4   Kittery's 1940 and 1950 population totals were 5,374 and 8,380; Portsmouth's were 14,821 and 18,830, respectively.
5   *The Portsmouth Herald*, "Boy is Safe," Feb. 3, 1934.

school then being returned home, had continued. Eventually, though, he had to stay permanently at the State Industrial School until he became an adult, at which time he'd only completed two years of high school.

That penal institution for youths had "pardoned" Joseph in 1942 so he could join the U.S. Army.[6] He'd enlisted on February 7, 1942, mid-World War II, at age 18.

He'd completed basic training at Fort Meade in Maryland and then had been stationed at Camp Roberts, California, where he'd been attached to the First Air Corps of the U.S. Army Air Forces. Consequently, he'd been moved to the Army infantry; it's unknown why, possibly as a disciplinary action for some indiscretion.

About 10 days following "V-J Day" ("Victory Over Japan Day"), which marked the end of WWII, Private Joseph L. Hardy, Jr. had been back at home, on his first military furlough in 3.5 years.

After 14 days' leave, he'd reported to Camp Croft, South Carolina for further assignment. While there, on September 20, 1945, he'd married Virginia Baptiste, a member of the U.S. Army's women's branch.

In October, with five months left to serve, according to his enlistment documents, Joseph had gone AWOL[7] from Camp

---

6   *The New York Times*, "Newlyweds Admit Hitchhike Murder," Aug. 5, 1947.

7   "AWOL" is the acronym for "absent without leave." If a service member is AWOL for 30 days, the offense becomes desertion, having acted upon the intent to leave one's assigned post permanently, which carries a penalty of dishonorable discharge, forfeiture of all pay and confinement of five years. In contrast, the punishment for being

Adair, Oregon because he "could not stand the militarization," he said.[8] Subsequently, he'd committed the military crime of desertion, as he never had returned to his assigned post. That had led to a bad conduct discharge in 1946.[9]

He would've been eligible for a military pension, as he'd served more than 90 days of active duty with at least one of them occurring during the eligible WWII time period between December 7, 1941 and December 31, 1946. It's likely he'd forfeited a pension by deserting but hadn't had to serve time for it.

In December 1945, Joseph had turned up in West Hartford, Connecticut, where he'd drunk heavily, a common activity for him. While intoxicated, he'd broken into and taken someone's car from Jensen's Gasoline Station. Also, he'd lifted some clothes from a guy in the Army who'd offered him a place to stay until he found a job.

Joseph had spent most of 1946 incarcerated. He'd begun the year by pilfering items from his parents' Kittery home, for which he'd gotten punished with six months' time in the York County Jail.

Upon his release in early summer, he'd been arrested again, this time for having stolen the automobile and clothes. He'd gotten a nine-month sentence in the Hartford County Jail for

gone for, say, three days, is a maximum one-month confinement and loss of two-thirds of pay for one month.

8   Joseph Hardy and Lois Hunt's written account from the Nevada County Jail, California, 1947.

9   Joseph Hardy's younger brother, Roger L. Hardy, also would go AWOL from the U.S. Army in 1953.

breaking and entering and three months, suspended, for theft.

While there, he'd served as a mess boy in the officers' quarters, a responsibility with some extra freedom only given to model prisoners.

Hartford County Sheriff Joseph W. Harding had described Joseph as a "quiet boy, never any trouble at all" but had noted he had "a quick temper and sometimes flared up with the inmates."[10]

In fact, Joseph had been released 45 days early, the maximum allowable, for his good behavior, in May 1947.

Soon after, though, he'd gotten into a violent brawl with someone, in which he'd sustained serious injuries. He'd been hospitalized for several days and after having been discharged, couldn't walk or, consequently, work.

"So I just hung around the town of Portsmouth," he said.[11]

During that idle time, he'd met Lois at the Jarvis Restaurant and Tea Room, where she'd worked as a waitress. "We fell in love and soon became inseparable," he said.[12] The two had gotten engaged, and Hardy had scored a job at Jarvis, too.

By mid-July, Lois had moved in with Joseph at his parents' home. When Hardy's self-described wanderlust had returned, he'd asked Hunt to go with him out west; she'd agreed.

---

10   *The Hartford Daily*, "Hardy Served in Local Jail as Mess Boy," Aug. 5, 1947.
11   Joseph Hardy and Lois Hunt's written account from the Nevada County Jail, California, 1947.
12   Joseph Hardy's written confession in Clark County, Nevada, Aug. 3, 1947.

After having pawned their belongings for a bit of cash, they'd set out, hitchhiking out of Maine, to begin their lives anew, together, elsewhere.

Now, on August 6, less than a month after Joseph and Lois had left the East Coast, their hearing concerning the murder of James McLain took place. It was held in the chapel of the local funeral home, the Truckee Mortuary, because the town's justice court couldn't accommodate all of the spectators.

This larger, makeshift courtroom, with a capacity of 75, was crowded with double that many onlookers, "some of whom leaned against coffins in an anteroom."[13]

Elsewhere in the building was James' body, which was to be shipped to Taft, California for a funeral and burial.

With Truckee Justice of the Peace R.N. Little presiding, District Attorney H. Ward Sheldon called CHP Officer Bill Gautsche and Sheriff Richard Hoskins as witnesses. He introduced the written statements of Lois and Joseph in Las Vegas, and presented photos of James McLain's body for identification purposes.

A signed statement of J.H. Bernard, M.D.,[14] Truckee's only physician, who'd performed the autopsy on James, was read aloud. It reconstructed the crime and described the condition of James' body when it'd been found.

---

13   *Reno Evening Gazette*, "Trial Ordered for Couple on Murder Charge," Aug. 7, 1947.

14   Dr. Bernard's office was located at 10104 Commercial Row, Truckee, upstairs.

Lois and Joseph, who'd waived legal representation for the proceeding, held hands, giggled, snickered and "showed little concern" throughout it.[15] Judge Little determined the couple was to be bound over for trial. After he announced this, Lois said to him, "I'll bet you think I'm a bad girl."[16]

Before and after their court appearance, the inmates chatted with reporters and posed for photos. Lois inquired of Hoskins if Joseph could join her in her cell, and he said no. She then asked Coroner Alvah Hooper, "Won't you come up with me?" Then she queried a reporter, "Don't you think I'm a sweet, innocent looking little girl?"[17]

Joseph told the newsmen, "We will make no defense of any kind in superior court. We plan to plead guilty," and noted that he and Lois wanted a quick legal resolution of their case.[18]

Subsequently, Hoskins drove the couple to the Nevada County Jail, about 55 miles to the west, to await the setting of their joint trial date. There, they would pass the time in large part by corresponding with each other.

Also during that period, Joseph wrote a letter to the jailer in Kittery, Deputy Sheriff Harland H. Welch, conveying he was ready for the consequences of his, and only his, recent "act." He thanked Welch for what he'd done for him during his time

---

15   *Reno Evening Gazette*, "Trial Ordered on Couple for Murder Charge," Aug. 7, 1947.

16   *The Sacramento Bee*, "Lure Slayers are Held to Answer Murder Charge," Aug. 8, 1947.

17   Ibid.

18   Reno Evening Gazette, "Trial Ordered on Couple for Murder Charge," Aug. 7, 1947.

in the York County Jail and said he "regretted not being able to show my appreciation by making good."[19]

---

19   *Portland Press Herald*, "Hardy Writes He's Ready for Penalty," Aug. 19, 1947.

8: ON THE RECORD

<u>August 7, Thursday</u>

When Raymond Hunt learned through the newspaper about James McLain's murder, he was "shocked" to learn his sister Lois was involved, he said.[1] He vowed to help her in any way he could.

The same day, Lois voluntarily submitted to questioning by D.A. H. Ward Sheldon and Sheriff Richard Hoskins, in the attorney's Nevada City office, excerpts of which follow. The transcript reveals that Lois sometimes was evasive, claiming she didn't know and, therefore, couldn't supply, many details.

She frequently deferred to Joseph, giving answers such as, "You will have to ask my husband" and "You could learn a heck of a lot more if you had my husband here."[2] In other instances, she contradicted herself.

---

1   *The Sacramento Bee*, "Brother in Vallejo Will Aid Lois Hardy," Aug. 7, 1947.
2   Lois Hunt's interview in Nevada City, California, Sept. 7, 1947.

THE ENDS

Lois recounted to Sheldon and Hoskins that James had "bothered her" and how he'd done so at the Sparks cabin when Joseph supposedly had left to buy beer.

Q: "What did McLain do?"

A: "That is an embarrassing question. I don't know exactly how to word it. He took me in his arms and kissed me. He had his arm around me and unbuttoned his pants and tried to pull me down on the bed with him. I just wasn't that kind of girl; he couldn't get anywhere with me. I gave him a shove. I told him to keep his hands off of me."

When Joseph had returned to the cabin, Lois had told him what James had done, and Joseph had gotten angry, she said. However, the couple had decided not to act until the next day.

Some of the officials' questions focused on her and Joseph's plans regarding James.

Q: "Did you intend to kill him when you got there, to that state park?"

A: "It says so there [in the statement made in Las Vegas]."

Q: "Is that right?"

A: "It must be."

Q: "Tell me, is it right or isn't it? Had you talked to your

44

husband about this?"

A: "I don't remember. I'm not going to answer any more questions until my husband is up here. I am not sure of any of this; I was angry at the time, boiling mad. When I get mad, I don't remember what I say or what I do."

Q: "You promised to give him your body at a more desolate spot?"

A: "Yes."

Q: "McLain thought he was going up there to have a good time with you, is that it?"

A: "Yes."

Q: "And Hardy knew about it?"

A: "I don't know."

Lois reiterated that McLain had wanted to have sex with her, and first had mentioned it during their initial car ride together, to Sparks.

Q: "You had talked about killing him before [the murder]?"

A: "I told my husband the night before that if he had left that gun there, the man at the foot of the bed, that fellow, wouldn't be alive."

45

While in bed after James allegedly had attacked her, Lois had intended to kill him, she said.

To questions about the day of and the murder of James, Lois responded:

Q: "When you went out [to Hirschdale] that day, you were planning on killing him?"

A: "If he got fresh again, I would."

Q: "Did you know he was going to get fresh? As a matter of fact, didn't you take him up there and tell him you would let him get fresh? Wasn't that how you got him up there?"

A: "I hate to talk anymore because I am only getting myself in deeper."

Q: "You have already told this in your [Las Vegas] statement."

A: "I've forgotten what is in it."

At another point during the questioning, Lois agreed that the Las Vegas statement was correct and true.

Sheldon probed the issues of premeditation and the extent of Lois' involvement.

Q: "Did you know your husband had the gun in his hand?"

A: "No, I didn't know when it was going to happen."

Q: "You knew it was going to happen."

A: "Yes, but I didn't know when. That is why I backed away so fast."

Q: "Didn't you pull [McLain's] head so that he couldn't see the gun?"

A: "One might have that impression."

Q: "Were you kissing him then?"

A: "Yes."

Q: "The main thing you wanted was to get that automobile, is that right?"

A: "No. To be perfectly frank with you, my mind was just flashing one thing: Who the hell does this old so-and-so think he is? Where does he get the idea he can have my body now or at any future date? I was madder than you ever saw any female get. I am also a wonderful actress when it comes to anything like that."

Q: "You had this whole thing planned since the night before?"

A: "Yes."

Q: "What do you expect is going to happen to you?"

THE ENDS

A: "Go to the gas chamber."

Q: "It doesn't seem to bother you."

A: "No. I just got out of the hospital a little over a year ago. They put me there because I tried to kill myself a couple of times."

Q: "How do you feel about killing McLain? Are you sorry for it?"

A: "Yes, very, not the idea of himself, just the idea that it was a human being."

Q: "You didn't think of that at the time?"

A: "No."

"I am as much to blame as my husband," Lois said. "I want the same punishment."

<u>August 8, Friday</u>

James McLain's family held a memorial service for him at the Erickson & Brown Funeral Home in Taft. He was buried in the West Side District Cemetery alongside his mother, Sarah Emma McLain, who'd passed away five years earlier at age 63.

When James was 28, he'd lost his father; George McLain had died in his early 50s in 1928. He, too, was buried in Kern County but in a different graveyard than his wife and son.

Surviving James were his sister Nola Marlatt, his brother-in-law Robert Marlatt and their children, Robert "Bobbie," 24, and Barbara Lee, 15.

Would justice, inasmuch as it could, be done for James?

9: LOVEBIRD FLIES AWAY

A t their arraignment in Nevada County Superior Court, Joseph Hardy and Lois Hunt reneged on their statements that they wouldn't seek counsel, wouldn't plead innocent and wouldn't put on a defense. They entered two pleas: innocent and not guilty by reason of insanity.

This meant they'd be tried twice, first to determine their guilt or innocence in the murder and, if found culpable, second, to establish their degree of sanity when they'd committed the crime.

Judge James Snell, age 69 and graying, denied bail for the defendants and set the trial date for roughly two months in the future, Monday, November 24. The couple was to be tried jointly.

In the meantime, Lois and Joseph would remain in the Nevada County Jail.

THE ENDS

September 19, Friday

Snell appointed three psychiatrists "to examine the defendants ... investigate their sanity, and to testify whenever summoned in any proceeding in which the sanity of the defendants or either of them is in question."[1]

They were Joseph Catton, M.D., private practitioner in San Francisco; R.B. Toller, M.D., superintendent of the Stockton State Hospital; and Walter Rapaport, M.D., superintendent of the Mendocino State Home, another mental health hospital.

October 10, Friday

Lois' current legal husband, Arthur G. Corliss, in Maine, learned about Lois and Joseph's crimes and marriage. He sought a divorce from her on the grounds of cruel and abusive treatment. It was granted.

Arthur and Lois only had lived together as a wedded couple for about three months, at which time Lois had moved out. Twenty-two days later, she and Joseph had embarked on their cross-country escapade.

November 17, Monday

It was one week before his and Lois' trial date when Joseph put into a motion a plan he'd hatched behind bars. At the time, he was being held with nine other inmates in what was called the jail's "big tank" on the second floor.[2]

---

1   Order Appointing Alienists, Sept. 19, 1947.
2   *Nevada State Journal*, "'Love Scene' Slayer Breaks From Prison," Nov. 19, 1947.

With a hacksaw blade he'd found under a sink in the institution, Joseph cut out one of the bars surrounding the prisoner holding tank on the second floor, crawled through it into the adjacent locked corridor and replaced the bar. He waited in the corridor until a deputy sheriff opened its outer door to admit a prisoner to the tank or take one out.

When that next happened, the deputy unlocked and opened the outer door, behind which Joseph hid. While the deputy was at the tank, Joseph slipped through the outer corridor door into a hallway and hid in a nearby, unlocked and empty cell.

When that same deputy later went up to the third floor, Joseph descended the stairs to the ground level, walked through the office and exited the building.

He was discovered missing the next morning. The last time anyone recalled seeing him was 4:30 p.m. on the previous day. None of the prisoners in the big tank "would or could give any clue to the method of escape."[3]

Sheriff Richard Hoskins was baffled as to how Joseph had disappeared and thought perhaps he was hiding somewhere in the facility. He launched a full-scale hunt for the inmate — supposedly wearing a light blue shirt and khaki pants — in the jail and throughout Northern California. Hoskins also considered that Joseph might stay in the area to attempt to free Lois, so he took precautions in that regard.

---

3   Ibid.

As for Lois, her "spirits dropped and she was cool in her references thereafter to Hardy."[4] Upset that her true love had abandoned her, she purposefully cut her left wrist. Whether it was for attention or a genuine attempt at ending her life is unknown.

Recovering, she told reporters, while sobbing, "I no longer have any love for Joey, but I'm not saying he's responsible for the trouble I'm in now. If there's any responsibility, it's to that controlling fate which brings an unwanted person into the world. Joey might have helped if he'd stayed. But he ran out on me. Never want to see him again. Thought he was the only person in the world who didn't want to hurt me."[5]

With Joseph on the lam, one trial of both defendants couldn't take place. Would it be delayed until his capture, assuming he was found? Or would it move forward anyway, for Lois alone?

December 4, Thursday

Two weeks and two days later, one of the Van Noy Interstate Company's chain of railroad terminal restaurants was robbed at about 10 p.m. It was in Sanderson, Texas, about 60 miles from the Mexico border. Items missing were $50 in cash, a camera and a rifle.

The manager suspected the culprit was the new guy, M.B. Bice, whom he'd hired 10 days earlier to work as a handyman

---

4   *Oakland Tribune*, "Second 'Kiss of Death' Trial to Open Monday," Jan. 17, 1948.
5   Reynolds, Ruth, *The Post-Standard*, "Justice Topsy-Turvy When Confusion Confounds Confessions," March 19, 1950.

and who was missing.

Law enforcement caught Bice trying to hop a freight car in the nearby railyard. When asked for identification, he presented a draft card that bore his name.

Officers had him remove his clothes to look for physical characteristics that would confirm his identity. They discovered Bice had a U.S. Army serial number tattooed on his arm, 11039289, which was assigned to Joseph L. Hardy, Jr.

Joseph was arrested on the spot as the suspect in the Van Noy and other recent burglaries around the area.

He'd stolen Bice's military document in the Nevada County Jail, where Bice, too, was an inmate. From Nevada City, the escapee had gone to Oakland then Los Angeles and finally The Lone Star State.

California authorities began the process of getting Joseph extradited back to their state to answer for the pending murder charge and now, another felony charge, of escaping from jail.

"It is apparent he was heading for the border, and it looks like he would have made it if he kept out of trouble," Hoskins said. "He is the type who cannot keep out of trouble."[6]

---

6   *The Sacramento Bee*, "Joseph Hardy, Lure Slayer, is Held in Texas," Dec. 5, 1947.

10: "RECKLESS, VIVACIOUS, SHREWD"

December 8, Monday

Joseph wasn't back in California yet, so a trial began for Lois only, for what newspapers referred to as "the sex lure slaying," "the embrace murder," "the death kiss slaying," "the mountainside caress murder," "the decoy killing" and/or "the kiss-of-death robbery slaying."

The courtroom, located on the building's third floor, was newly refurbished and boasted a modernistic flair. The judge's bench was waterfall style, and the counsel table was semi-circular. Behind that was a similarly shaped press table. The courtroom and a spectator section each contained 50 blue leather seats and featured green carpeting.

At the start of *The People of the State of California v. Lois Hunt Hardy*, the room was filled to seating capacity. James McLain's sister and brother-in-law, Nola and Robert Marlatt, were among the crowd of watchers.

THE ENDS

With Judge James Snell presiding, the attorneys quickly chose five women and seven men for the jury, examining only 57 of 100 prospects. Of those selected, all of the men and two of the women were from Nevada City. The remaining three women lived in Grass Valley. No Truckee residents qualified for the panel. Alternates weren't selected.

During voir dire, "Mrs. Hardy, although appearing nervous, laughed and talked with her [court-appointed] attorney," Lynne Kelly.[1]

Age 52, Kelly had been practicing civil law since 1919, first in San Francisco then Grass Valley, after two years of active duty in the U.S. Navy during World War I and an honorable discharge. This was Kelly's first murder case.

The prosecutor, Vernon Stoll, a Red Bluff, California native, recently had assumed the role of Nevada County district attorney following the sudden passing of H. Ward Sheldon, 40, on September 25 due to a heart ailment. Stoll, age 44, had run a law practice in Grass Valley for the previous two decades.[2] Though he'd been the D.A. in 1942, this was Stoll's first murder trial, too.

As for Lois, "if pitiful appearance could have freed this pale and nervous blonde she would never have gone into a courtroom. Her arms and legs were like pipe stems," a reporter described.

"Her face, particularly around her sunken cheeks, was

1   Nevada State Journal, "Jury Chosen in Truckee Slaying Case," Dec. 9, 1947.
2   Eventually, Vernon Stoll would take Judge James Snell's place upon his retirement in 1958 and would serve in that capacity until 1968, when he would become a visiting judge in Northern California.

suggestive of a death mask. Her deep-set eyes were lifeless. The black dress Lois wore was thoroughly unsuitable both to her complexion and her predicament. It was black net, low necked and trimmed with ribbon. The 90-pound girl looked like a dejected wallflower at a party — D.A. Stoll's party."[3]

December 9, Tuesday

In his opening remarks, Stoll asserted that Lois and Joseph had lured James into the woods, where they'd "disposed of him" and "after doing so, had ransacked his person" for valuables.[4]

CHP Officer Harold Fowler took the stand. He testified to having reached the crime scene by having taken a side road off of Highway 40 to its end then having continued on foot.

He said that just after 7:15 p.m., in a clearing surrounded by brush and jack pine trees, he and the other searchers had found the corpse of a man, aged 55 to 60, 190 pounds, covered with a blanket and already decomposing. A small blue mattress or pad had lain a few feet away.

Truckee Constable "Tom" Dolley testified to his search of and findings at the crime scene and his removal of James' body.

Sheriff Richard Hoskins spoke to the arrest of Lois in Las Vegas and his transporting her and Joseph to Northern California.

Coroner Alvah Hooper said that during that trip, he'd sat in

---

3   Reynolds, Ruth, The Post-Standard, "Justice Topsy-Turvy When Confusion Confounds Confessions," March 19, 1950.
4   The Sacramento Bee, "Lois Hardy Faces First Witnesses in Lure Murder Trial," Dec. 9, 1947.

the back seat of Hoskins' vehicle and had conversed with the two prisoners flanking him.

Hooper described one incident during the travel in which Lois had pointed to a spot and had said, "We were going to shoot him down there but it was too close to the highway." The coroner also testified that he and Hoskins had taken the couple to the murder location, and Lois had confirmed, "Yes, that's the place."

J.H. Bernard, M.D., who'd conducted the autopsy, testified about his findings and the state of James' body when retrieved.

David Q. Burd, California Bureau of Investigation criminologist, identified the recovered gun as a French-made Unique 7.65 mm automatic pistol and the two recovered spent cartridge shells as being 0.32-caliber Remington UMC.

Stoll admitted several items as evidence. Ones from the crime scene were the cartridge cases, the bloody rock, a red robe and a 2x5-foot blue mattress. Also admitted were the gun, James' car title, autopsy pictures and photographs, found in James' vehicle, in which Robert Marlatt identified his brother-in-law.

When the prosecutor showed the postmortem images and the murder weapon in court, Lois turned her head to avoid looking at them.

Next, the first legal skirmish between the attorneys began. It was over the admission of two records. Stoll wanted them in; Kelly didn't. One was Lois' confession in Las Vegas, which Kelly asserted wasn't Lois' because she hadn't handwritten it herself (she'd dictated it to Joseph). The other was the transcript of her interview later by now deceased D.A. Sheldon and Hoskins.

December 10, Wednesday

Snell ruled the Las Vegas confession was inadmissible because it was believed to be Joseph's, not Lois'. Because it'd been used as the basis for the questioning of Lois in Nevada City, Snell denied admittance of the second document as well.

Stoll, however, worked around those limitations. He got the information contained in the Las Vegas statement revealed to the jury through the testimony of Clark County Sheriff's Deputies "Butch" Leypoldt and Alexander Kennedy about the substance of their questioning of Lois.

The admitted exhibits were Bank of America travelers cheques #63 to #69, discovered at the Boulder Highway car accident site.

December 11, Thursday

Stoll and Kelly argued the admissibility of testimony from Gladys Dolley, the woman to whom Lois spoke openly in the Truckee Jail. Though Kelly purported that anything Lois had told Gladys had been done so under duress and coercion, the prosecution prevailed in that battle.

Gladys, 34, took the stand. She testified she'd been acting as the jail matron on the night that Lois had been placed there, Aug. 5, 1947.

THE ENDS

After Hoskins had asked her to find out what she could from Lois about the bloody cloth-wrapped stick, she and the stenographer, Vivian Alice Gregory, had gone to Lois' cell. Gladys had entered, but Gregory hadn't.

Gladys said she'd asked Lois what the stick and handkerchief had been used for. Lois had said she couldn't recall but might remember if she could tell the whole story of the murder-robbery of James, which she did, from concoction to execution.

Lois had admitted to having participated, Gladys testified. Lois said she'd nodded to Joseph when it was a good time for him to execute James. "I held him in my arms while Joe shot him," Gladys quoted Lois as having told her.[5] Lois had demonstrated on Gladys how exactly she'd done it. The first bullet hadn't killed James, Lois had said, so Joseph had shot him again.

Gladys had asked Lois if she'd been afraid she'd be shot accidentally. She replied that she hadn't been because of her full confidence in Joseph's ability.

Lois also had confessed to the lipstick on James' face being hers and her having used the stick to stuff Joseph's handkerchief into James' mouth.

December 12, Friday

Gregory corroborated Gladys' entire account.

The People rested.

---

5   *The Sacramento Bee*, "Truckee Matron's Story Links Lois Hardy to 'Lure' Slaying," Dec. 12, 1947.

Kelly opened for the defense, saying, "We will show that Lois Hardy is a weak person mentally who is easily influenced by other people. We will show the crime was entirely conceived and executed by [Joseph] Hardy without any cooperation, connivance or assistance from this defendant.

"We will show that if she did any acts in connection with the crime that she did so unknowingly and unwittingly. We will show that she is an innocent person who weakly became a tool in the hands of a murderer, Joseph L. Hardy, Jr."[6]

December 15, Monday

The defense's star witness, Lois, took the stand.

"Did you kill James McLain," Kelly asked her.[7]

"Not to my knowledge," Lois answered in a whisper. "I might have killed him."

"Did you hold his head and direct the killing?"

"Not intentionally."

"Do you know whether you took part in the killing at all?"

"No."

"Did you lure McLain to the spot where he was killed?"

"Not intentionally."[8]

---

6   *The Sacramento Bee*, "Lois Hardy is to Enter Denial, Tell Life Story Monday," Dec. 13, 1947.
7   *Nevada State Journal*, "Lois Hardy to Testify Next Week," Dec. 13, 1947.
8   Ibid.

THE ENDS

Despite speaking quietly during her testimony, Lois appeared calm and even laughed occasionally, but she never made eye contact with the jurors.

In testifying about her earlier life in New England — she'd been born in New London, Connecticut on April 21, 1925 — she described having been an "unwanted" child and, thus, having gotten passed off from relative to relative until her teens.[9]

"I guess I might best be called a misfit in life," Lois said. "I never had the security of a home or a mother's love. And as far as men are concerned, I've been disillusioned, from my father to Joe Hardy. The only memory of my [biological] father was that of a beast. I never learned what happened to him."[10]

When Lois had been nine months old, her mother had sent her to stay with Lois' grandmother in Florida, she said, because Lois' father allegedly had avowed that "he would have my body before any other man would."[11]

At age four, Lois had been taken to live with her maternal aunt and her husband, whom she'd thought were her parents, in Louisville, Kentucky, which 1930 U.S. Census records confirm.

Lois had said in her interview with Sheldon and Hoskins that she'd resided with those relatives until age 13 or 14. However,

---

9   Reynolds, Ruth, *The Post-Standard*, "Justice Topsy-Turvy When Confusion Confounds Confessions," March 19, 1950.
10   Ibid.
11   *The Union*, "Accused Woman Claims She Doesn't Remember Anything About Death," Dec. 15, 1947.

census records show that at age 10 and 15, in 1935 and 1940, respectively, Lois had been living in New London with her mother Julia G. Heavilin,[12] stepfather Samuel S. Heavilin and brother Raymond Hunt.

Lois told the jury, "I heard my mother say once, 'If Lois were a boy I could love her, but she looks too much like her father.' Then I found out [Samuel] was my stepfather and not my real father although he was swell to me."[13]

When Lois had been 17, with only two years of high school completed, she'd married Walter Peret, a 20-year-old Connecticut mechanic, on June 3, 1942. She told of always having argued with Peret, still having been a virgin three months after their wedding, his having been drafted into the service in 1945 and her having gone to live with his mother. The two ladies hadn't gotten along, so Lois had gone to Portsmouth, after which she'd stayed "in bed for one full month," she said.[14]

A few years after the Perets' nuptials, the couple had sought and had been granted a divorce.

In March 1946, at age 21, Lois again had gotten married, this time to Arthur G. Corliss, who'd been 17 years her senior. That union had been even shorter than Lois' first, the two having cohabitated for fewer than three months, due to "elderly"

---

12   Julia Heavilin (maiden name Smith) gave birth to Raymond Hunt in 1923 at age 20 then to Lois Hunt in 1925 at age 22. In 1930, at age 27, Julia married Samuel Heavilin, age 31, in what was at least her second marriage.
13   *The Union*, "Accused Woman Claims She Doesn't Remember Anything About Death," Dec. 15, 1947.
14   Ibid.

Arthur's jealousy.[15] This second husband had accused Lois of going out with his best friend, which she'd adamantly refuted.

The defendant testified to a 3.5-month period in her life, between September and December 15, 1946, of which she had no memory. She next remembered having been enrolled in the Hartford Hospital School of Nursing. Later, she'd dropped out due to reportedly having suffered a nervous breakdown, for which she'd been hospitalized.

"They put me there because I tried to kill myself a couple of times," she said.[16] In here first attempt, she'd drunk a bottle of lighter fluid, and in the second, she'd consumed another equally ineffective substance. She told the jurors she more recently had tried to take her life while in the Nevada County Jail.

After Lois had been released from the hospital, she'd worked in a gambling club in New London for some time. After, she testified, she'd stayed in a rooming house and had waitressed at the Jarvis Restaurant and Tea Room, both in Portsmouth. It was at Jarvis that she'd met Joseph and had "found happiness."[17]

Soon after, she'd quit her job and had moved in with him. Two weeks later, the couple had left Kittery.

December 16, Tuesday

---

15   Reynolds, Ruth, *The Post-Standard*, "Justice Topsy-Turvy When Confusion Confounds Confessions," March 19, 1950.

16   Lois Hunt's interview in Nevada City, California, Sept. 7, 1947.

17   Ibid.

As for her recall of James' murder, Lois testified she had none and that wasn't unusual because she'd suffered amnesic episodes throughout her life. She and Joseph hadn't planned to rob or hurt James, she claimed.

She relayed the story she'd told Sheldon and Hoskins of James having hugged her in his car while Joseph drove and of her having repeled James. In court, though, she embellished it, adding that later in the drive, when James had been back at the wheel, she'd fallen asleep on Joseph's shoulder but had woken to find herself leaning on James and his arms around her.

She further stated that after she, Joseph and James had arrived at the Sparks cabin, Joseph had stepped out to get some beer. "Soon as he left, McLain came towards me, he put his arms around me, kissed me, and I pushed him away because I didn't want him to do that. I told him if he lay his hands on me again, I'd kill him. But I don't think I did because I didn't have anything to kill him with," she said.[18]

Her next vague remembrance, she added, was of being "in the woods and being pushed down and down."[19] What she recalled next was having been alone in James' car after the accident in Southern Nevada.

Her knowledge of what had happened during the time in between, she asserted, was limited to what Joseph had

---

18   *The Union*, "Accused Woman Claims She Doesn't Remember Anything About Death," Dec. 15, 1947.
19   *Nevada State Journal*, "Memory Lapse in Shooting Case Claimed," Dec. 16, 1947.

relayed to her afterward, and her participation in any of the intervening events had been "unknowing and unintentional."[20] She claimed Joseph had instructed her to repeat the story exactly as he'd told it to her, when anyone asked what had happened.

As for her having confessed to Gladys in the Truckee Jail, Lois claimed she'd made up the story she'd told her about the handkerchief and stick because she'd thought Gladys was a newspaper reporter.

Regarding the time she'd spent in the Nevada County Jail before her trial, Lois testified she'd "kept her chin up" until Joseph had escaped.[21] When she'd learned her illegal husband had abandoned her, she'd begun to cut her wrists, but a deputy sheriff had caught and stopped her.

"I don't think I can hold out much longer," she added. "I still love Joey and will 'til the day I die but will never go near him again."[22]

Next, Joseph Catton, M.D., one of the psychiatrists who'd evaluated Lois, testified. He said Lois had told him she'd shot James; she'd remembered taking the gun out of her belt as he was attacking her and shooting him. That account differed from the one she'd told the jury just the day before and the one she'd relayed before her trial.

Catton said that Lois, when he evaluated her again the

---

20   Ibid.
21   *The Union*, "Accused Woman Claims She Doesn't Remember Anything About Death," Dec. 15, 1947.
22   Ibid.

previous day, admitted having lied to him.

His opinion, he said, was that Lois' amnesia was a so-called "pretense and not a defense."[23] Catton went on, "She is an actress and, admittedly, I believe there is more truth yet untold and that she knows more about the tragedy than she is telling. She is an entirely different person here today than when I examined her."

He explained that he never before had seen Lois' type of amnesia, "a blankness which was unbroken."[24] He said it was possible, but unlikely, that shock from recent events caused her memory loss.

Catton described Lois as "neurotic but not insane," conceited and having "enjoyed the battle of wits" with the doctors.[25]

In Lois' defense, however, he said that after reading all of the letters between Lois and Joseph, he believed Joseph had been the mastermind behind the crime and had told Lois what to say and how to act.

Following Catton, Lois again took the stand. She admitted she'd lied to the psychiatrists and her attorney.

"I wove a pattern of lies, but now I've told the truth," she testified. "It was all Joey's fault. You probably won't believe me because I'm like the boy who cried 'wolf.'"[26]

---

23   *The Union*, "Hardy Case to Go to Jury Tomorrow," Dec. 17, 1947.
24   Ibid.
25   Ibid.
26   Reynolds, Ruth, *The Post-Standard*, "Justice Topsy-Turvy When Confusion Confounds Confessions," March 19, 1950.

Lois said she'd trusted Joseph fully until he'd escaped from jail. She would've done anything, even if wrong, that he'd asked her to. Now, though, she doubted everything that came out of his mouth, she said, and when she thought about all that he'd told her, she found "little lies that seem obvious."[27]

December 17, Wednesday

Kelly testified that Lois had told him only one account of the events, the one she'd relayed in court, and never had wavered from it.

Next, the attorneys made their closing remarks. In his, Kelly asked the jury to acquit Lois, as she merely had been Joseph's "tool."[28]

Stoll concluded with: "Due to all the stories told here by Lois Hunt Hardy, I am confused on all but one thing — that this defendant and Joseph Hardy killed McLain. Are we trying the innocent, demure and truthful Lois Hardy or the reckless, the vivacious, the shrewd?"[29]

December 18, Thursday

The judge instructed the jurors and told them they had to decide on one of four outcomes. They were first degree murder, which carried a punishment of death or life imprisonment; second degree murder, the penalty for which was five years to life; manslaughter, with a sentence of one to 10 years in

27   *The Union*, "Hardy Case to Go to Jury Tomorrow," Dec. 17, 1947.
28   *Nevada State Journal*, "Hardy Trial Nearing End," Dec. 18, 1947.
29   Reynolds, Ruth, *The Post-Standard*, "Justice Topsy-Turvy When Confusion Confounds Confessions," March 19, 1950.

prison; or acquittal.

The jurors retired for deliberations at about 2:20 p.m. Three votes and nearly two hours later, they reached a verdict.

By that time, Joseph had been extradited and was back in the Nevada County Jail. However, because he'd been placed in solitary confinement on his return, he didn't learn of Lois' fate until the day after it was announced in court.

The body of her peers found Lois guilty of the first degree murder of James W. McLain and did not recommend clemency!

The "no mercy" component of the jurors' determination was unusual and unexpected because Stoll hadn't requested they return a death sentence recommendation. Because the jury did, though, it made capital punishment mandatory in the case, which at the time in California was execution by lethal gas, carried out at San Quentin Prison.[30]

In other words, Snell, by law, had no choice but to sentence Lois to death, assuming a conviction in her upcoming, associated sanity trial. Kelly made a motion to move forward with the insanity proceeding, and Snell continued his ruling on it until December 19.

Despite the outcome calling for her death, Lois remained seemingly calm after hearing it in court, however, on her way

---

30   After the state would kill prisoner Robert Alton Harris in the 1990s, a federal court would declare that execution by lethal gas was unconstitutionally cruel and unusual. Subsequently, the gas chamber at San Quentin would be altered to facilitate deaths with a different method, lethal injection.

back to the Nevada County Jail, she sobbed. Once back in her cell, she was placed on suicide watch.

"It's rather ironical because several years ago I tried to commit suicide, and they placed me in a hospital," she later told the press. "Now I'm going to have a chance to die with my boots on."[31]

December 19, Friday

In court, Kelly changed his tack. He withdrew Lois' insanity plea and his motion for an insanity trial.

He then requested a brand new trial in accordance with California Penal Code 1181. It allowed a defendant convicted of a crime to seek a new trial if, during their previous one, any of the grounds, or incidents of judicial wrongdoing, outlined in the statute applied. Kelly claimed all of them did.

Snell set January 2, 1948 as the date to hear arguments for and against a new trial.

December 26, Friday

Joseph was arraigned on the jail breaking charge and held to answer in superior court. Bail was set at $5,000. Were Hardy to be convicted on the murder charge, he wouldn't be tried for his escape.

What would the outcome of his trial be?

---

31   *Nevada State Journal*, "Killers Tell Sordid Story," Aug. 5, 1947.

11: FIGHT FOR LIFE

<u>1948</u>

<u>January 2, Friday</u>

Defense Attorney Lynne Kelly presented nine statutory reasons why Lois Hunt deserved a new trial.

1) Lois had been tried in absentia, in the local newspapers, and the public had considered her guilty before she even had gone to trial.

As proof, Kelly read two editorials, one each from different newspapers. He read three postcards sent to himself, Judge James Snell and D.A. Vernon Stoll, all containing the same opinion that Lois was being pampered and, instead, should be put to work at hard labor to "earn back for the county the money spent on her trial."[1]

---

1   *The Sacramento Bee*, "Lois Hardy Opens Fight to Resist Death Penalty," Jan. 2, 1948.

Another letter, one to Sheriff Richard Hoskins and signed by "The Committee of 12" claimed its members had reviewed the evidence against Lois and had concluded she was guilty. They'd asked for administration of "speedy justice."[2]

2) The jury had gotten evidence outside of the courtroom and had to have known about the adverse public sentiment toward Lois.

Kelly introduced affidavits from two jurors in which they'd described strangers outside the court trying to discuss the case with them.

One juror, Chester Peterson, had been telephoned and asked to "meet a committee"[3] on Commercial Street the next day, but he hadn't. After the subsequent court session, someone had driven past him and had asked, referring to the requested rendezvous, "Why didn't you show up?"

Also, a woman had approached Angelina Falconi in the meat market and had asked her if she was a juror. Falconi had replied that yes, she was, but she wouldn't discuss the case. The woman had retorted, "When you are through, your reputation may not be so good."[4]

3) The jury had been guilty of misconduct, which thereby had prevented them from fairly considering the case. Kelly claimed all of the jurors, except one perhaps, had believed, when they'd been sworn in, Lois was guilty.

---

2 Ibid.
3 Defendant's Points and Authorities on Motion For a New Trial, Jan. 7, 1948; *People v. Hardy*, 33 Cal.2d 52, scocal.stanford.edu.
4 Ibid.

This was evidenced, he said, by none of them having expressed any doubt about her guilt or the presumption of her innocence; the jury's first vote had been unanimous for a verdict of first degree murder. The severity of the verdict also showed the jurors' predisposition.

When Peterson had told a deputy sheriff about the attempts to intimidate and influence him and, thus, his concern for his family and his property's safety, Kelly had taken the issue to the court. In response, Snell had offered to declare a mistrial, but Stoll had declined. Lois hadn't been informed of the decision or given the chance to agree or disagree with it.

"It may here be noted that the attorney appointed by the court to act for said defendant had no authority to decline such offer to declare a mistrial and that the same was done without the knowledge or consent of the defendant," Kelly said.[5]

4) The verdict had been decided unfairly, in this case by lot, or by chance without a logical evidential basis.

Kelly purported the actions of a self-described "citizens committee," which had deemed Lois guilty before a trial, had influenced how the judge had conducted the trial and how the jury had voted.[6]

5) The court had misdirected the jurors in matter of law, by having refused to give them certain instructions, having modified other directions and having provided further ones that were faulty.

---

5   Ibid.
6   Ibid.

6) The court had erred in its decision concerning a question of law.

Snell's order directing the reading of a portion of Clark County Deputy Sheriff's Alexander Kennedy's testimony, which Snell later had deemed inadmissible, had been wrong and prejudicial to Lois. Further, when Snell had corrected the mistake later, his doing so had "fixed the inadmissible evidence more firmly in the minds of the jurors."[7]

7) The prosecutor had been guilty of prejudicial conduct in front of the jury several times.

Kelly claimed Stoll had made an unfair opening argument and had misstated the evidence in his closing comments.

8) Evidence had been insufficient to support the verdict, and further proof, material to Lois, had been discovered since the verdict, which couldn't have been found prior to and produced at the trial.

For instance, Kelly argued that identification of the cartridge cases, the gun and even James had been inconclusive. Further, defense counsel noted that all of Lois' confessions and admissions had been false entirely and had conflicted with the objective evidence.

Stoll countered every one of Kelly's points, insisting all procedures had been followed correctly and the trial had been unbiased.

---

7   Ibid.

January 8, Thursday

With "a blank and fixed smile on her lips, Lois sat in the courtroom awaiting Snell's determination."[8]

He ruled against her, denying the motion for a new trial.

Accordingly, punishment on the conviction immediately followed. Snell sentenced Lois to death by lethal gas at the hand of the state, at San Quentin.

She remained silent for a bit then turned to Kelly and said, "Oh, please don't look like that. Don't look downhearted or I'll bust out crying."[9] She shook hands with Stoll and then Kelly. Then, appearing emotionless, she left the courtroom with a jail matron.

Because her case involved capital punishment, Lois was guaranteed an appeal to the California Supreme Court, per state law.

Were the higher court to uphold the lower court's ruling, Lois would be the third woman to be executed by lethal gas since the state had adopted the method in 1937 to replace hanging.

To carry out death in the new manner, cyanide crystals were mixed with sulfuric acid and distilled water to create a deadly gas, which then was diffused through the chamber in which the dead man (or woman) walking was placed. Needing to

---

8   *Portland Press Herald*, "Lois Hardy Sentenced to Gas Chamber Death," Jan. 9, 1948.
9   Reynolds, Ruth, *The Post-Standard*, "Justice Topsy-Turvy When Confusion Confounds Confessions," March 19, 1950.

breathe, the condemned prisoner inhaled the vapors that then caused his or her demise.

Lois soon would learn her fate.

12: RECKONING FOR JOSEPH

January 9, Friday

Lois Hunt was transferred to the California Institution for Women in the city of Tehachapi,[1] which housed female death row inmates. Rather than cells, the penitentiary housed women in cottages, each with sleeping quarters, a kitchen and a dining room.

Ironically, the facility was located on an isolated mountain site in Kern County, the region in which James McLain had spent much of his life and where he currently was interred.

As for Joseph Hardy, it now was his turn to be tried for first-degree murder. In advance of his trial, his court-appointed attorney Frances "Frank" G. Finnegan moved to have the matter dismissed because it hadn't been tried within 60 days of the charge being filed.

---

1   Until 1937, the facility had been called Tehachapi and had been San Quentin State Prison's branch for women. The name had been changed when it split from San Quentin but still was referred to often as Tehachapi.

Finnegan, 41, bald and bespectacled, practiced law in Nevada City. He'd been admitted to The State Bar of California in 1930 and, like his client, was a World War II veteran.

Judge James Snell denied the motion and set a trial date: January 19, 1948.

Finnegan then withdrew Joseph's previous guilty by reason of insanity plea, leaving only the one of innocence on the record.

January 16, Friday

A week later, Joseph appeared in court alone for arraignment on the jailbreaking charge. He stated he didn't have and didn't want counsel, and he pleaded guilty.

Snell continued the matter to January 30.

January 19, Monday

The People of the State of California v. Joseph L. Hardy, Jr. began. Throughout the trial, Joseph appeared calm and neat, with his hair combed, his suit and striped tie, both blue, ironed and his shoes shined.

Jury selection began and continued into the next day.

January 20, Tuesday

Finnegan and D.A. Vernon Stoll excused about 100 prospective jurors primarily because they already had decided Joseph was guilty. As such, Snell had a special venire summoned of 30 people from Nevada City and Grass Valley. Most of the six women and six men chosen for the jury came from that group.

80

Finnegan made his initial remarks. He said he'd show that the Hardys hadn't been alone in the forest area in which James had been shot on July 30, 1947.

Stoll, on the other hand, reserved the right to make his opening statement later. Instead, he began calling witnesses.

The trial proceeded much like Lois' did at first. CHP Officer "Bill" Gautsche, Truckee Constable "Tom" Dolley and Dr. J.H. Bernard testified, and Stoll presented the same exhibits.

January 21, Wednesday

Similarly, Sheriff Richard Hoskins, Coroner Alvah Hooper, Criminologist David Burd, Robert Marlatt and Clark County Deputy Sheriffs Alexander Kennedy and "Butch" Leypoldt all again took the stand.

Toward the end of the day in court, Stoll and Finnegan argued for about an hour over admissibility of the statement Joseph had written out in Las Vegas.

January 22, Thursday

Finnegan asserted that Leypoldt had obtained Joseph's confession under inducement when he'd told him and Lois it would "help them if they told the truth."[2] Snell, though, determined that hadn't constituted an incentive and, thus, the statement was admissible.

Stoll read a segment of it into evidence. The prosecutor bolstered the document's impact by following it with

---

2   *Nevada State Journal*, "Judge Allows Lure Murder Confession," Jan. 24, 1948.

Kennedy's testimony about its contents.

Kennedy said Joseph and Lois had been warned their statement would have to be free and voluntary and might be used against them. He denied that he, Leypoldt or anyone else had made threats or promises to either suspect when trying to obtain each of their stories surrounding the crimes.

Kennedy also testified to having called law enforcement in Reno, Nevada after having learned about the murder of James. Kennedy had put Joseph on the phone to describe the body's exact location and how to get to it.

January 23, Friday

Recalled to the stand, Hoskins relayed that while transporting the Hardys to Truckee from Las Vegas, Joseph had said he'd stopped at a bar and had liked the alcoholic drink he'd ordered. He'd relayed this when the caravan had been in Hirschdale.

Jesse H. Strickland, proprietor of that place, testified that in the afternoon of the day of the murder, Joseph had come into his establishment and had ordered and left with a whiskey.

Counsel argued the admissibility of Joseph and Lois' "account of what has come to pass and its contributing factors," referred to in court as the "Life Story," which the two had collaborated on while in the Nevada County Jail. Joseph had written it down, and both he and Lois had signed it. Because it was undated, it's unknown whether they'd created it before or after the late D.A. H. Ward Sheldon and Hoskins had questioned Lois in Nevada City.

Despite Finnegan's objections, Snell allowed the part related to the murder to be admitted into evidence and read aloud in court.

The narrative contained some new variations of prior divulgences. One was the claim that when James had picked up Lois and Joseph at the Utah-Nevada border, he'd asked Joseph to drive. After getting back on the road, James, in the back seat with Lois, allegedly had become "rude and forward with Lois. Once I stopped and demanded an explanation but he only laughed and called it a joke," Joseph had written.[3]

Another pertained to the events of the night before the crimes.

According to Joseph, "[James] did not annoy Lois again until we reached our cabin at Sparks. He sent me off to get some beer and upon my return he was in the shower and Lois was crying. She said he had tried to force himself upon her and only by great effort was she able to resist his advances. I was greatly perturbed and loaded our gun, which heretofore had been empty. I fully planned to kill him at once but Lois talked me out of it, saying it would be suicide in such a compact surrounding. I finally gave in, and the evening and night passed uneventfully."

The document also described the couple's current attitude:

"We do not expect or desire sympathy in any form. We fully realize the seriousness of our offense and stand prepared to pay for it in any way the State of California may direct.

---

3   Joseph Hardy and Lois Hunt's written account from the Nevada County Jail, California, 1947.

"Lois and I are not afraid of the consequences. We are ready to meet our Lord because we know he has forgiven us and is ready to welcome us into His great domain. ... We have talked with God and have accepted him as our Savior. We are ready to meet him."

Joseph and Lois had cited their lackluster childhoods as the reason for their crimes against James. The pair had described Joseph's youth in detail but only had made a few points about Lois', that she once had been hospitalized for a nervous breakdown "and is at present a very sick girl."

The explanation went on, "We were not always wayward nor do we beleive [sic] we were destined to become murderers. Had we been alloted [sic] the simple privileges of the average youngster in our early years we would no doubt today be respected and honorable members of our communities."

The duo had ended their account with a plea to the public to not neglect their children, which they'd called criminal, and, instead, to supervise and support them.

Next, in court, it was the defense's turn to present its case, but Finnegan didn't call any witnesses.

Both sides rested.

January 26, Monday

Stoll presented his opening statements, highlighting in them that Joseph had confessed to the crime.

Finnegan, in his closing arguments, focused on the case's

emotional aspects and, several times, mentioned Joseph's comment, "I wanted to back out, but Lois said if I wouldn't [shoot James], she would do it herself."[4]

Further, in an apparent plea to the jurors to not find Joseph guilty of first degree murder, Finnegan reminded them that "the Army teaches its men to kill."[5]

Stoll got in the last word, telling the jury, "I think you will be justified in returning a verdict the most severe the law provides."

<u>January 27, Tuesday</u>

The jurors deliberated from roughly 11 a.m. to 4 p.m. and took an hour for lunch in between.

They returned a verdict of guilty of murder in the first degree and recommended life imprisonment.

"Hardy showed considerable emotion at the reading of the verdict, it not carrying the gas chamber sentence that his wife had received in December."[6]

After wiping his eyes, he shook hands with Finnegan and Stoll and left the courtroom smiling.

Lois' reaction was, "I'm glad, very, very glad. Joey is a very lucky boy, but he's the kind of guy who always comes thru [sic] all right." She expressed surprise that Joseph, with a

---

4   Reynolds, Ruth, *The Post-Standard*, "Justice Topsy-Turvy When Confusion Confounds Confessions," March 19, 1950.

5   *Portland Press-Herald*, "No Witnesses Offered for Joseph Hardy," Jan. 27, 1948.

6   *The Union*, "Hardy Sentence to Life to be Fixed Tuesday," Jan. 28, 1948.

criminal record, had received a life in prison recommendation from his jury while she, with a clean past, had gotten a death recommendation from hers.

Back in his cell, Joseph told newsmen the plan to kill James was all his own, and Lois hadn't known about it. To support those claims, he gave yet another description of how the murder of James came about.

"While we drove along, with Lois dozing in the back seat," Joseph said, "I asked McLain if he could go for Lois.[7] He said he could, and I said maybe I could arrange it. When I finally turned off the road, Lois wanted to know what the idea was. I drove into the clearing, and taking a blanket and a radio out of the car, I winked at McLain to follow.

"I told Lois to remain in the car as I wanted to talk over some business with the old guy," Joseph continued. "We walked about 500 feet to where I spread the blanket and turned on the radio, meanwhile telling McLain I would do a vanishing act after telling Lois to come over.

"He chuckled and said, 'Don't take too long, kid.' I answered, 'Don't worry, Mac, I won't,' and let go with the first shot. As the gun blasted, Lois came darting out of the car, screaming, 'Oh, Joey, what have you done?' After that she kept saying, 'Joey, we're in this together, and no matter what happens we'll stick together.'"[8]

---

7   Reynolds, Ruth, *The Post-Standard*, "Justice Topsy-Turvy When Confusion Confounds Confessions," March 19, 1950.
8   Ibid.

Joseph also said he'd been stunned when Lois had blurted out during the Clark County Jail revival service that she had a confession. She'd consoled him, though, by saying, "Just stick with me, Joey, and we'll cause so much confusion, I'll save you!"[9]

On the same day as Joseph's verdict, across the country, in Alfred, Maine, a judge granted Joseph's actual wife, Virginia Hardy, an annulment of their September 20, 1945 marriage.

Virginia had filed for it on September 12, 1947, two months after Joseph and Lois had commenced their journey westward.

On the petition, Virginia had written that when she and Joseph had wed, she hadn't known he had a criminal background. She only had learned of his penchant for trouble with the law when, after they'd become husband and wife, he'd gotten convicted of and had served time for robbery. The two hadn't lived together ever.

January 30, Friday

Because Hardy now had been found guilty of murder, he didn't have to stand trial for his jailbreak. For that charge, Snell sentenced him to imprisonment at San Quentin State Prison for the time period dictated by law.

February 3, Tuesday

Snell again meted out punishment for the convicted felon, this time for murdering James — a life term behind bars. The

---

9   Ibid.

two sentences were to be served concurrently.

Joseph received the news "without any emotion and without comment."[10]

February 5, Thursday

He began his incarceration at the "Big Q."

Joseph told the press he predicted Lois would receive a new trial and be acquitted. He believed he, as well, ultimately would be freed, and he and Lois would "go on from there."[11]

A few days later, he requested a copy of his and Lois' marriage certificate. He wrote that he wanted it for "sentimental reasons"[12] but couldn't pay for it because he was behind bars.

February 29, Sunday

Lois lost her brother Raymond Hunt, 24, in a plane accident. At the time of his passing, he'd been flying with a friend near Napa, California, practicing "power of gliding spirals."[13] At some point, Raymond allegedly had miscalculated their altitude and had been unable to recover in time. The plane had crashed, killing only him.

Was the death of Lois, too, imminent?

---

10   *The Sacramento Bee*, "Joseph Hardy is Sentenced to Life in San Quentin," Feb. 3, 1948.
11   *Oakland Tribune*, "'Kiss of Death' Killer Starts Life Sentence," Feb. 5, 1948.
12   *The Sacramento Bee*, "Hardy Gets 'Sentimental' And Writes for Copy of Marriage Certificate," Feb. 7. 1948.
13   *The Sacramento Bee*, "Body of Lois Hardy's Brother, Plane Victim, Goes East for Burial," March 2, 1948.

13: REPRIEVE GIVEN

November 1, Monday

After four months of considering the appeal concerning Lois Hunt's conviction and death penalty sentence, the Supreme Court of California reversed both. It ordered she be afforded a new trial on the first-degree murder charge because her initial trial had been a miscarriage of justice.

The jurists cited several reasons for their decision. One was that Lois' testimony, despite having been legally sufficient, though contradictory, had provided "weak support for a judgment imposing the extreme penalty."[1]

Additionally, the court concluded Judge James Snell had made various judicial errors in the trial related to admitting evidence and directing the jury. For instance, in some instances, he'd provided information to jurors that he shouldn't have; in others, he'd withheld it wrongly.

---

1   *People v. Hardy*, 33 Cal.2d 52, scocal.stanford.edu.

Further, some of the instructions Snell had given during the trial conflicted with one another. He erroneously had evidence re-read to the jury that he earlier had stricken from the record and had allowed the attorneys to repeat prohibited statements in their closing arguments.

The Supreme Court justices wrote that they hadn't needed to consider the threats to the jurors because the trial errors alone had warranted an overturned judgment.

While Lois awaited her new trial, Joseph continued his punitive confinement at San Quentin. His mother told the press that Junior, what his family called him, routinely wrote letters to her and her husband.

In one of them, he mentioned he'd been taking high school classes with the goal of finishing those and moving on to advanced courses.

With Joseph's future certain, Lois' would be decided early in the next year.

14: JUSTICE SOUGHT AGAIN

<u>1949</u>

<u>January 24, Monday to January 28, Friday</u>

About two years after the conclusion of her original trial on the first degree murder charge related to the slaying of James McLain, Lois Hunt was back in the Nevada County Jail for a do-over.

The players this time around mostly were the same as before — Judge James Snell, D.A. Vernon Stoll and Defense Attorney Lynne Kelly. What differed was the addition of co-counsel to the defense at Kelly's request.

He was Albert Lawrence Johnson, age 62. Brown eyed, bald and of medium build, he was "a forceful yet quiet and unassuming speaker."[1]

---

1   Tinkham, George Henry, *History of Stanislaus County*, Historic Record Company: Los Angeles, 1921.

THE ENDS

After having being admitted to The State Bar of California in 1909, Johnson had worked 40 years as an attorney in San Francisco, Modesto and Oakland before Nevada City. His uncle was former California governor and U.S. senator, Hiram W. Johnson.

For this second case of *The People v. Lois Hunt Hardy*, the attorneys on both sides selected seven women and five men for the jury, from a list of 250 candidates.

Lois, wearing a black dress and a short bob hairstyle, sniffled from a cold.

"Colorless, and without the advantage of makeup, the skinny defendant appeared to have lost the weight that brought her up to a husky 82 pounds while at Tehachapi last year."

At the start, Snell ruled several items inadmissible. They included any and all testimony that was given in Lois' first trial. They also included conversations with Lois and Joseph that had taken place in the Clark County Jail and in the car ride from there to Truckee.

The defense asked that all people not connected with the case be excluded from the court. Snell granted the request.

The D.A. delivered his opening argument, "citing briefly the first trial."[2] Again, the same individuals — Harold Fowler, "Bill" Gautsche, Richard Hoskins, "Tom" Dolley, Alvah Hooper and Robert Marlatt — testified, repeating what they'd

---

2   *The Sacramento Bee*, "Presentation of Evidence Begins in Hardy Retrial," Jan. 25, 1949.

said in the previous trials, of Lois and Joseph.

Snell made an exception to his earlier ruling and allowed the prior testimony of Dr. J.H. Bernard to be read into the record.

Clark County Sheriff's Deputies Alexander Kennedy and "Butch" Leypoldt took the stand but were restricted in their testimony to what Joseph and Lois had told them about having used James' car.

Kelly tried, unsuccessfully, to get Truckee Jail matron, Gladys Dolley, excluded from testifying because, as a newspaper had concluded in the past, "[Her testimony] was the most telling blow in the state's case against Mrs. Hardy" in her initial trial."[3] Kelly again argued that Lois' alleged confession to Gladys had been obtained illegally and under "duress and oppression" and that Lois had been detained in the Northern California facility unlawfully.

On the stand now, Gladys reiterated what she'd testified to previously. She said Lois had begun with, "We went up a little road by a bridge, walked through the brush to the side of a hill. We had a radio, blanket, mattress and a bottle of wine."[4]

Gladys noted that Lois had read Bible passages as she'd relayed how she'd lured James to the remote location on the promise of sex with her.

Lois had divulged, Gladys said, that after the shooting, the blood oozing from James' face had made her queasy. To

---

3   Ibid.
4   *The Union*, "Court Admits Testimony of Dolley," Jan. 28, 1949.

stanch the flow, "I took a handkerchief out of Joe's pocket and stuffed it in the man's mouth," Lois had said.[5]

At the end of their conversation, according to Gladys, Lois had told her, "I'm glad you came up and let me talk. God will forgive me and receive me."[6]

Gladys testified she wholeheartedly believed Lois' statements to her in the Truckee Jail were true and did not believe Joseph had pressured Lois to confess.

Kelly, in his cross-examination of Gladys, aimed to discredit her testimony by showing it differed from the version she'd given at Lois' first trial. Kelly accused Gladys of both embellishing her account and omitting certain details from it. He asked her why she'd given information in this trial that she hadn't provided in the previous one.

She answered that she'd been called late at night just before the first trial to appear as a witness and had been "too excited. Now, I have had time to straighten it out in my mind."[7] Kelly, however, implied that she remembered more details now because she, in the interim, had discussed the case with others or had read about it.

Kelly asked Gladys, "Didn't it seem implausible that a young girl like Lois would kiss a man like James?"

"No," she answered.

---

5   Ibid.
6   *The Fresno Bee*, "Matron Says Lois Admitted Luring McLain to Death," Jan. 28, 1949.
7   *The Union*, "Court Admits Testimony of Dolley," Jan. 28, 1949.

Following Gladys' appearance, the People rested.

Johnson moved for a not guilty verdict on the grounds the state hadn't provided sufficient evidence of Lois' guilt. Snell denied the motion.

Kelly presented the defense's opening statement. He would attempt to show, he said, that Lois hadn't been in California at the time of the murder. If he failed to do that, he would, at the least, demonstrate that the prosecution's case left room for reasonable doubt.

The defense's opening witness, Jesse H. Strickland, testified that on the day of the murder, Joseph had entered Strickland's bar alone, bought a whiskey and left. Strickland never had seen Lois, he said.

January 31, Monday

Both sides argued the admissibility of Joseph Hardy's criminal record, which included petty larceny, theft and two charges of desertion from the U.S. Army. Snell allowed it in, and Hoskins read it to the jury.

Then, as in her 1947 trial, Lois took the stand. When she relayed the events leading to the crime, she again changed them. In this latest telling, she claimed the night before the murder, James had raped her in the Sparks cabin in which she and Joseph had been staying the night with him.

Yet, on cross-examination, she said she couldn't remember if she'd been sexually assaulted or not.

She recalled James undoing his pants and "trying to kiss me and push me down," she said. "[I] slapped him and told him to keep his hands off me or I'd kill him. That's all I remember."[8]

She added that this interaction with James caused her to black out immediately and remain in that state through the murder-robbery, through her subsequent gambling and drinking in Reno afterward, through the hours-long drive to Las Vegas and through her marriage to Joseph and subsequent celebration, until the automobile crash on the Boulder Highway.

"I did not participate in the killing of McLain in any way, as far as I know," she said.[9]

When Stoll showed Lois pictures of James' dead body, she covered her eyes and said, "No, no. Please take them away."[10] She'd reacted similarly when she'd been tried the previous year.

Lois testified that Joseph had instructed her to "get his story of the killing word for word and not to change it," so she'd memorized it and had told it to Gladys that very way because she'd "wanted to do anything to save Joe's neck."

The defendant said she didn't recall the bloody stick and handkerchief and didn't remember much about the trip to Truckee from Las Vegas because "everything was shimmering around me."[11]

---

8   Reynolds, Ruth, *The Post-Standard*, "Justice Topsy-Turvy When Confusion Confounds Confessions," March 19, 1950.
9   *Nevada State Journal*, "Lure Suspect Says Slaying Was Justified," Feb. 1, 1949.
10   *Portland Press Herald*, "Death Penalty Not Asked at Hardy Trial," Feb. 2, 1949.
11   *The Union*, "Hardy Trial Nears Finale; Defense Rests," Feb. 1, 1949.

On the stand, she again told the story of her childhood and having been passed from relative to relative.

"There was no kindness with my mother and stepfather, and I didn't feel wanted," Lois said. "One of the first to show me real, unselfish affection was Joey."

She'd met him in summer 1947 at the tea room where she'd worked, she relayed.

"Joey came in, and he looked hungry and forlorn. I found out that he was broke so I fed him and paid for his meals whenever he came in after that," she said.[12]

She detailed her and Joseph's cross-country trip and described having been miserable throughout it.

"I didn't understand the crazy setup," she said, "but I was in love with him and I went along. Joe made no effort to find a job."[13]

<u>February 1, Tuesday</u>

The final defense witness, Harold L. Karo, M.D. from Grass Valley, bolstered Lois' amnesia claim. Karo was a U.S. Army physician who'd seen soldiers in combat overseas experience memory loss.

He explained to the jury that amnesia was the temporary loss of memory, either partial or complete, and that it was caused by a brain injury, shock to the nervous system or disease.

---

12   Ibid.
13   Ibid.

Karo added that amnesia victims may have only a hazy, confused impression of previous events, they typically don't recall their blackout periods and they often blame forgetfulness for their inability to remember them.

"It would be possible for a girl who had been assaulted by a large man to suffer nervous shock or injury and that she could witness the shooting of a man and later fail to remember it," Karo testified.[14]

The defense rested its case.

Stoll, in his closing argument, asked the jurors to find Lois guilty but didn't ask them to recommend the death penalty.

Johnson delived final remarks on Lois' behalf. He underscored that Lois hadn't been responsible for her actions with James because she'd been suffering from shock at the time, shock that had resulted from James' sexual assault of her.

"This innocent woman was attacked by a criminal who got his just desserts. She was under the domination of the murderer who had been a criminal since he was 11 years of age," he added, referring to Joseph.[15]

February 2, Wednesday

Snell gave the jurors numerous instructions. They should give credibility to Lois' testimony in court, he told them.

To find Lois guilty of first degree murder, they must be

---

14   *Long Beach Independent*, "Waitress in 'Kiss of Death' Slaying Freed," Feb. 3, 1949.
15   Ibid.

convinced beyond a reasonable doubt that she participated in the "willful, deliberate and premeditated" murder of James, Snell clarified.

He continued, "If you find that on July 30, 1947, the defendant was assaulted by James McLain and suffered shock resulting in amnesia, and did not remember the events that followed, the law comes to her aid and presumes that she was not guilty of the crime.

"If you believe the evidence shows the conscious mind of the defendant ceased to operate and her actions were controlled by the subconscious or subjective mind," Snell added, "you are instructed to return a verdict of not guilty."[16]

The jurors deliberated for an hour then returned with a "general surprise"[17] in the way of a verdict.

They found Lois not guilty!

She sobbed on hearing the words.

"I feel wonderful," she told reporters. "I prayed every night. Now I know the Lord answers prayers."[18]

When Joseph, a little over one year into his sentence, received the news of Lois' exoneration, he said, "I'm the happiest guy in this whole prison."[19]

---

16   The Sacramento Bee, "Lois Hardy is Acquitted in Second Trial," Feb. 2, 1949.

17   The Portsmouth Herald, "Lois Hardy's 'Prayers Answered,' Wins Freedom in 'Lure' Slaying," Feb. 3, 1949.

18   The Bakersfield Californian, "Lois Hardy Wins Freedom; Credits Prayer," Feb. 3, 1949.

19   Oakland Tribune, "San Quentin," Feb. 3, 1949.

THE ENDS

Courtroom observers opined that Karo's testimony and Snell's indirect reference to Lois' mental state clinched the verdict.

An opinion piece in *The Sacramento Bee* called Lois' acquittal "a rank miscarriage of justice." It went on: "So Lois goes scot free. And society can only hope her subconscious and subjective mind does not cut up any more [sic]. Tommyrot!"[20]

An "Irate Taxpayer" in Grass Valley seconded the editor's stance, writing, "You undoubtedly expressed the sentiment of at least 95 per cent [sic] of the residents of this county." The letter continued, "Something went wrong somewhere, and many of us would like to know what it was."[21]

---

20   *The Sacramento Bee*, "Miscarriage of Justice," Feb. 4, 1949.
21   *The Sacramento Bee*, "Letters From the People — The Lois Hardy Trial," Feb. 14, 1949.

EPILOGUE

After Joseph Hardy served 28 years and nine months and after at least eight, perhaps more, denied requests for parole, the California Department of Corrections (CDC) released him from San Quentin State Prison. During his stint that ended in November 1976, his parents passed away, his father in 1954, his mother in 1969.

After regaining his freedom, Joseph married a divorcée with two adult daughters, and the couple settled down in Santa Cruz, a Northern California coastal city. There, they managed a Best Western motel and lived in a nearby mobile home community.

Joseph served on the executive board of the Beach Area Business Association and was a member and one-time president of the California Motel Association's local chapter. He occasionally suggested, in letters to the *Santa Cruz Sentinel*, changes that he believed would help attract tourists and visitors to the area.

THE ENDS

The CDC lifted the ex-convict's parole in July 1980. Joseph was 57.

Twelve years later and 16 years after leaving prison, on November 11, 1992, Joseph expired at age 69 while in Reno, Nevada, presumably on a trip there. A private funeral was held for him, and his body was cremated.

About 200 miles away, back in Nevada County, where James McLain had been murdered and robbed, Lois died at age 67, on October 19, 1992, three weeks before Joseph did.

Within a few years of her acquittal, Lois married one of her attorneys, Albert L. Johnson, who was 39 years her senior. She took his last name and went by either "Lois," or "Joyce," or sometimes a combination of the two, "Lois Joyce" or "Joyce Lois."

The Johnsons resided in a 4,000-square-foot, two-story house on Nevada City's main thoroughfare and had a son in 1954. Lois was a homemaker, and Albert practiced law long past retirement age. He still was working at age 88.

Albert passed away at age 95 in 1981, and his remains were cremated.

In 1986, Lois sold her and Albert's house. The following year, the Nevada County public guardian became the conservator of Lois and her estate, likely because she no longer was able to care for herself fully. Eventually, Lois grew ill from pyelonephritis, inflammation of the kidneys caused by a bacterial infection, which persisted for several years.

She was living in a skilled nursing rehabilitation facility in Grass Valley at the time of her demise, which occurred at Sierra Nevada Memorial Hospital nearby. Sepsis caused her death; the medical condition resulted from the infection moving into her bloodstream and, in doing so, turning fatal.

Lois' cremated remains were buried in Nevada County's Penn Valley Cemetery. At the site, the Nevada Cemetery District provided a temporary headstone bearing the name Joyce Lois Johnson and the years she lived. That original marker remains there today because, contrary to custom, no one ever replaced it with a permanent one.

PHOTOGRAPHS

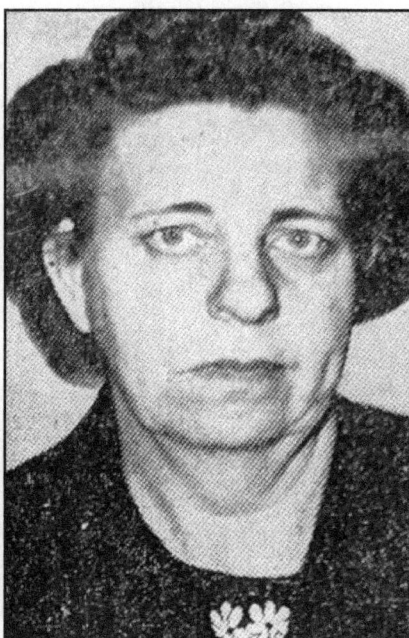

James W. McLain, left; Nola Marlatt, his sister

Joseph L. Hardy, Jr. and Lois Hunt

1947 Ford Sedan, James' year and style of car

Joseph L. Hardy, Jr. and Lois Hunt

Nevada County, California, blacked out area

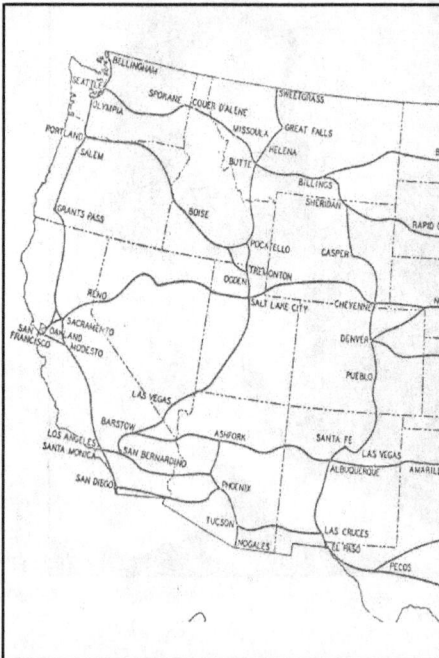

Western U.S. interstates, 1947

Truckee Jail register, names and page numbers

Adjacent cells in the Truckee Jail, today a museum

William "Bill" Gautsche

J.H. Bernard, M.D. and Richard W. Hoskins

Alvah Hooper

"Tom" F. Dolley and Harold B. Fowler

Gladys Dolley

W.E. "Butch" Leypoldt

Alexander H. Kennedy

Lois Hunt

Joseph L. Hardy, Jr.

Joseph L. Hardy, Jr. and Lois Hunt

Joseph L. Hardy, Jr. and Lois Hunt

James W. McLain

SOURCES

Berkeley Daily Gazette (Calif.), "Accused Slayer in Escape From Prison," Nov. 18, 1947.

Berkeley Daily Gazette (Calif.), "'Confession' Told in Trial," Dec. 11, 1947.

Berkeley Daily Gazette (Calif.), "Hope Held For Killer's Return," Nov. 19, 1947.

Berkeley Daily Gazette (Calif.), "'Lure' Killer Faces New Murder Trial," Jan. 24, 1949.

Berkeley Daily Gazette (Calif.), "'Lure' Slayer May Get Life Imprisonment," Jan. 28, 1948.

Berkeley Daily Gazette (Calif.), "'Lure' Slayer to Get Chair," Jan. 8, 1948.

Berkeley Daily Gazette (Calif.), "'Lure' Slayer Wins Appeal," Jan. 8, 1949.

Berkeley Daily Gazette (Calif.), "Murder Trial Opens Today," Dec. 9, 1947.

Berkeley Daily Gazette (Calif.), "Newlyweds in State to Face Killing Charge," Aug. 5, 1947.

Berkeley Daily Gazette (Calif.), "Pair Confess Murder in Jail Revival," Aug. 4, 1947.

Berkeley Daily Gazette (Calif.), "Slay Suspect Held in Texas," Dec. 5, 1947.

Death certificates of Joyce Lois Johnson and Albert L. Johnson.

El Paso Herald-Post (Texas), "Bride Who Confessed at Jail Revival Faces Trial," Aug. 5, 1947.

Find A Grave index, findagrave.com.

Joseph Hardy and Lois Hunt's written account from the Nevada County Jail, 1947.

Joseph Hardy's written confession in Clark County, Nevada, Aug. 3, 1947.

Letters of Conservatorship for Joyce Lois Johnson.

Lois Hunt's interview in Nevada City, California, Sept. 7, 1947.

Long Beach Independent (Calif.), "Confessed Killer Gets Out of Jail," Nov. 19, 1947.

Long Beach Independent (Calif.), "Couple Lures Man to 'Kiss of Death,'" Aug. 5, 1947.

Long Beach Independent (Calif.), "'Death Kiss' Retrial Looms," Nov. 3, 1948.

Long Beach Independent (Calif.), "Waitress in 'Kiss of Death' Slaying Freed," Feb. 3, 1949.

Long Beach Independent (Calif.), "Wife Found Guilty of 'Lure'

Slaying," Dec. 19, 1947.

Los Angeles Times (Calif.), "Confessed Killers Seek Attorney," Aug. 6, 1947.

Los Angeles Times (Calif.), "Confession Told in Death of Missing Man," Aug. 4, 1947.

Los Angeles Times (Calif.), "Psalm Singing Leads to Murder Confession," Aug. 5, 1947.

Macaulay, Tom, *Sierra Sun*, "Ghosts of the Truckee River Canyon; Once Bustling Towns Gone but Not Forgotten," Dec. 19, 2001, sierrasun.com.

MacCormick, Austin H., *New Hampshire State Industrial School, Manchester, A Survey Report*, New York, 1943, babel.hathitrust.org.

Naugatuck News (Conn.), "Life Sentence Faces Maine Man Convicted in California Death," Jan. 28, 1948.

Nevada Marriage Index, 1956-2005.

Nevada State Journal, "Death Sentence," Jan. 11, 1948.

Nevada State Journal, "Giggling Killers are Now in Jail at Nevada City," Aug. 8, 1947.

Nevada State Journal, "Hardy Couple Enter Plea," Sept. 17, 1947.

Nevada State Journal, "Hardy Trial Jury Panel is Drawn," Jan. 13, 1948.

Nevada State Journal, "Hardy Trial Nearing End," Dec. 18, 1947.

Nevada State Journal, "Honeymooning Killers Held in Truckee," Aug. 6, 1947.

Nevada State Journal, "Joseph Hardy Trial Opens; Jury Studied," Jan. 20, 1948.

THE ENDS

Nevada State Journal, "Judge Allows Lure Murder Confession," Jan. 24, 1948.

Nevada State Journal, "Judge Takes Hardy Case Under Study," Jan. 4, 1948.

Nevada State Journal, "Jury Chosen in Truckee Slaying Case," Dec. 9, 1947.

Nevada State Journal, "Jury Finds Hardy Guilty; To Get Life Imprisonment," Jan. 28, 1948.

Nevada State Journal, "Killers Tell Sordid Story," Aug. 5, 1947.

Nevada State Journal, "Lois Hardy Asks Another Jury Trial," Dec. 20, 1947.

Nevada State Journal, "Lois Hardy Guard Set," Dec. 24, 1947.

Nevada State Journal, "Lois Hardy to Testify Next Week," Dec. 13, 1947.

Nevada State Journal, "'Love Scene' Slayer Breaks From Prison," Nov. 19, 1947.

Nevada State Journal, "Lure Slaying Confession Given Jurors," Jan. 23, 1948.

Nevada State Journal, "Lure Slaying Tale Related to Jury," Dec. 12, 1947.

Nevada State Journal, "Lure Suspect Says Slaying Was Justified," Feb. 1, 1949.

Nevada State Journal, "Memory Lapse in Shooting Case Claimed," Dec. 16, 1947.

Nevada State Journal, "Memory Loss Theory Hit During Trial," Dec. 17, 1947.

Nevada State Journal, "Murdered Man's Checks Are Found," Aug. 13, 1947.

Nevada State Journal, "Nevada City Police Can't Locate Hardy," Nov. 20, 1947.

Nevada State Journal, "Nevada County D.A. Stricken Suddenly," Sept. 26, 1947.

Nevada State Journal, "Slaying Gun is Located," Sept. 24, 194.

Nevada State Journal, "State Opens Hardy Trial," Jan. 21, 1948.

Nevada State Journal, "Trial Date Set on Murder Charge," Sept. 21, 1947.

Nevada State Journal, "Trial of Hardy Set January 19," Jan. 10, 1948.

Nevada State Journal, "Trial Ordered for J. Hardy," Dec. 28, 1947.

Nevada State Journal, "Two Testify at Lure Trial," Dec. 11, 1947.

New Hampshire Marriage Records, 1637-1947.

Oakland Tribune (Calif.), "Doomed Woman's Appeal Before Court," June 9, 1948.

Oakland Tribune (Calif.), "'Kiss of Death' Killer Starts Life Sentence," Feb. 5, 1948.

Oakland Tribune (Calif.), "'Kiss of Death' Slayer Guilty," Jan. 28, 1948.

People v. Hardy, 33 Cal.2d 52, scocal.stanford.edu.

Portland Press Herald (Maine), "Death Penalty Not Asked at Hardy Trial," Feb. 2, 1949.

Portland Press Herald (Maine), "Hardy, Bride Feel Sure of Execution," Aug. 6, 1947.

Portland Press Herald (Maine), "Hardy Defense Puts up Battle," Jan. 22, 1948.

Portland Press Herald (Maine), "Hardy Writes He's Ready for Penalty," Aug. 19, 1947.

Portland Press Herald (Maine), "Jury Finds Hardy Guilty But Rules Out Execution," Jan. 28, 1948.

Portland Press Herald (Maine), "Jury Seated For Trial of Joseph Hardy," Jan. 21, 1948.

Portland Press Herald (Maine), "Lois Hardy Sentenced to Gas Chamber Death," Jan. 9, 1948.

Portland Press Herald (Maine), "Lois Hunt Hardy Again Faces Jury," Jan. 25, 1949.

Portland Press Herald (Maine), "Lois Hunt Hardy to be Retried," Dec. 7, 1948.

Portland Press Herald (Maine), "No Witnesses Offered for Joseph Hardy," Jan. 27, 1948.

Reno Evening Gazette (Nev.), "Accused's Story Told Before Jury," Jan. 28, 1949.

Reno Evening Gazette (Nev.), "Appeal is Won by Lois Hardy," Nov. 2, 1948.

Reno Evening Gazette (Nev.), "Awaits Trial," Jan. 26, 1949.

Reno Evening Gazette (Nev.), "Jury Frees Lois Hardy," Feb. 3, 1949.

Reno Evening Gazette (Nev.), "'Kiss of Death' Woman is Sued," Oct. 11, 1947.

Reno Evening Gazette (Nev.), "Kiss Lure Death Retrial is Set," Jan. 8, 1949.

SOURCES

Reno Evening Gazette (Nev.), "Lois Hunt Hardy Return Ordered," Dec. 3, 1948.

Reno Evening Gazette (Nev.), "Nevada News of the Year From Gazette's Daily Files," Dec. 31, 1948.

Reno Evening Gazette (Nev.), "Officers Testify for Hardy Trial," Jan. 27, 1949.

Reno Evening Gazette (Nev.), "The Hardy Trials," Nov. 3, 1948.

Reno Evening Gazette (Nev.), "Trial Ordered for Couple on Murder Charge," Aug. 7, 194.

Reno Evening Gazette (Nev.), "Truckee Hearing for Hitchhiker and His Bride," Aug. 6, 1947.

Reno Evening Gazette, "Verdicts Unpredictable," Feb. 3, 1949.

Reynolds, Ruth, *The Post-Standard* (N.Y.), "Justice Topsy-Turvy When Confusion Confounds Confessions," March 19, 1950.

Santa Cruz Sentinel (Calif.), "Obituaries—Joseph L. Hardy," Nov. 19, 1992.

The Bakersfield Californian, "Kiss Death Victim Rite Set in Taft," Aug. 5, 1947.

The Bakersfield Californian, "Lois Hardy Wins Freedom; Credits Prayer," Feb. 3, 1949.

The Bakersfield Californian, "Lure Slayer to Get New Trial," Dec. 8, 1948.

The Bakersfield Californian, "Matron's Story Related Today," Jan. 28, 1949.

The Bakersfield Californian, "Murder Hearing Set in Mortuary," Aug. 6, 1947.

THE ENDS

The Bakersfield Californian, "Newlywed Couple Ask Swift Trial in McLain Death," Aug. 7, 1947.

The Bakersfield Californian, "Second Murder Trial to be Set," Jan. 6, 1949.

The Bridgeport Post (Conn.), "Accused Killer Sought," Nov. 20, 1947.

The Daily Review (Calif.), "Jury List Selected in Murder Trial," Jan. 14, 1949.

The Daily Review (Calif.), "Jury Retires Today in McLain Murder," Feb. 2, 1949.

The Daily Review (Calif.), "Lois Hardy Acquitted of 'Lure' Murder," Feb. 3, 1949.

The Des Moines Register (Iowa), "Wife, Who Lured Victim, and Slayer in Suicide Pact," Aug. 5, 1947.

The Evening Independent (Ohio), "Married Less Than a Week, Held for Murder," Aug. 4, 1947.

The Express (Pa.), "Bride Couple Held in Murder," Aug. 5, 1947.

The Hartford Daily Courant (Conn.), "132 Persons on Superior Court Docket," Sept. 14, 1946.

The Hartford Daily Courant (Conn.), "Court Hands Down Prison, Jail Terms," Sept. 20, 1946.

The Hartford Daily Courant (Conn.), "Hardy Served in Local Jail as Mess Boy," Aug. 4, 1947.

The Hartford Daily Courant (Conn.), "Town Court," Aug. 22, 1946.

The Miami News (Fla.), "Husband Describes How Blonde Wife Embraced Victim in Woodland Slaying," Aug. 4, 1947.

124

SOURCES

The New York Times, "Newlyweds Admit Hitchhike Murder," Aug. 5, 1947.

The People of the State of California v. Joseph Leslie Hardy, Jr. and Lois Hunt Hardy, also known as Mrs. Joseph L. Hardy, number 8856.

The People of the State of California v. Joseph L. Hardy, number 8931.

The Portsmouth Herald (N.H.), "Accident Report," July 1, 1953.

The Portsmouth Herald (N.H.), "Accidents," June 23, 1952.

The Portsmouth Herald (N.H.), "Boy is Safe," Feb. 3, 1934.

The Portsmouth Herald (N.H.), "Bradley Sharman Struck By Car," Sept. 20, 1948.

The Portsmouth Herald (N.H.), "Flames Damage Homes in Kittery," Nov. 3, 1953.

The Portsmouth Herald (N.H.), "Four Local Youths Enlist in U.S. Army," March 2, 1942.

The Portsmouth Herald (N.H.), "Funeral Notices," Jan. 29, 1954.

The Portsmouth Herald (N.H.), "Kittery," Feb. 18, 1929.

The Portsmouth Herald (N.H.), "Kittery," Jan. 29, 1954.

The Portsmouth Herald (N.H.), "Kittery Soldier Held on AWOL Charge," May 22, 1953.

The Portsmouth Herald (N.H.), "Local Cars in Collision," May 23, 1927.

The Portsmouth Herald (N.H.), "Lois Hardy Awaits Gas Death Verdict," Oct. 22, 1948.

The Portsmouth Herald (N.H.), "Lois Hardy's 'Prayers Answered,' Wins Freedom in 'Lure' Slaying," Feb. 3, 1949.

THE ENDS

The Portsmouth Herald (N.H.), "Mattress Blaze on Parker Place," Nov. 9, 1934.

The Portsmouth Herald (N.H.), "Obituaries," Nov. 24, 1939.

The Portsmouth Herald (N.H.), "Personal Mention," July 16, 1952.

The Portsmouth Herald (N.H.), "Police Arrest Man on Kittery Warrant," Jan. 5, 1946.

The Portsmouth Herald (N.H.), "Police Court," May 26, 1934.

The Portsmouth Herald (N.H.), "Pvt. Hardy Home After Three Years," Aug. 25, 1945.

The Portsmouth Herald (N.H.), "Roger L. Hardy Enlists in Army," Sept. 8, 1951.

The Portsmouth Herald (N.H.), "Superior Court Grants Divorces," Feb. 13, 1946.

The Portsmouth Herald (N.H.), "Three Cars in Crash on Road at Stratham," May 18, 1934.

The Sacramento Bee (Calif.), "120 Are Summoned for Lois Hardy Trial Jury," Jan. 19, 1949.

The Sacramento Bee (Calif.), "Appeal of Lois Hardy Death Decree is Filed," April 13, 1948.

The Sacramento Bee (Calif.), "Births Recorded—Johnson," Sept. 1, 1954.

The Sacramento Bee (Calif.), "Body of Lois Hardy's Brother, Plane Victim, Goes East for Burial," March 2, 1948.

The Sacramento Bee (Calif.), "Bridal Couple Lure Man to Death in Hills," Aug. 4, 1947.

The Sacramento Bee (Calif.), "Brother in Vallejo Will Aid Lois

Hardy," Aug. 7, 1947.

The Sacramento Bee (Calif.), "Counsel is Named to Defend Lure Slayers," Sept. 6, 1947.

The Sacramento Bee (Calif.), "Defense Files for New Trial for Lois Hardy," Dec. 20, 1947.

The Sacramento Bee (Calif.), "Defense Moves to Break Lois Hardy Link With Killing," Jan. 29, 1949.

The Sacramento Bee (Calif.), "Defense Rests in Lois Hardy Trial for McLain Death," Feb. 1, 1949.

The Sacramento Bee (Calif.), "Dinner Changes Because Lawyer, 88, Will Stay on Job," Oct. 18, 1974.

The Sacramento Bee (Calif.), "Gun Used in Kiss Murder is Found," Sept. 23, 1947.

The Sacramento Bee (Calif.), "Hardy Confession is Admitted Into Evidence at Trial," Jan. 22, 1948.

The Sacramento Bee (Calif.), "Hardy Gets 'Sentimental' and Writes for Copy of Marriage Certificate," Feb. 7, 1948.

The Sacramento Bee (Calif.), "Hardy is Arraigned on Jail Break Charge," Dec. 27, 1947.

The Sacramento Bee (Calif.), "Hardy is Sentenced on Jail Break Count," Jan. 30, 1948.

The Sacramento Bee (Calif.), "Hardy is Taken to San Quentin Prison," Feb. 4, 1948.

The Sacramento Bee (Calif.), "Hardy Pleads Guilty to Jail Break Charge," Jan. 16, 1948.

The Sacramento Bee (Calif.), "'Innocent' Blonde Bride Tells of

Truckee Robbery Slaying," Aug. 4, 1947.

The Sacramento Bee (Calif.), "Jan 24th is Set For Lois Hardy Trial," Jan. 7, 1949.

The Sacramento Bee (Calif.), "Joseph Hardy is Sentenced to Life in San Quentin," Feb. 3, 1948.

The Sacramento Bee (Calif.), "Joseph Hardy, Lure Slayer, is Held in Texas," Dec. 5, 1947.

The Sacramento Bee (Calif.), "Judge Rules Out Confessions in Hardy Trial," Dec. 10, 1947.

The Sacramento Bee (Calif.), "Jury Deliberates Fate of Hardy in Murder Trial," Jan. 27, 1948.

The Sacramento Bee (Calif.), "Jury is Selected in Murder Trial of Joseph Hardy," Jan. 20, 1948.

The Sacramento Bee (Calif.), "Key Witness is Cross Examined in Hardy Trial," Jan. 28, 1949.

The Sacramento Bee (Calif.), "Letters From the People—The Lois Hardy Trial," Feb. 14, 1949.

The Sacramento Bee (Calif.), "Lois Hardy Case Nears Jury, State Opens Argument," Dec. 17, 1947.

The Sacramento Bee (Calif.), "Lois Hardy Faces Death Penalty By Jury's Verdict," Dec. 19, 1947.

The Sacramento Bee (Calif.), "Lois Hardy Faces First Witnesses in Lure Murder Trial," Dec. 9, 1947.

The Sacramento Bee (Calif.), "Lois Hardy Gives Changed Story in Murder Trial," Jan. 31, 1949.

The Sacramento Bee (Calif.), "Lois Hardy Gives Vague Replies to

State's Questions," Dec. 16, 1947.

The Sacramento Bee (Calif.), "Lois Hardy is Acquitted in Second Trial," Feb. 2, 1949.

The Sacramento Bee (Calif.), "Lois Hardy is to Enter Denial, Tell Life Story Monday," Dec. 13, 1947.

The Sacramento Bee (Calif.), "Lois Hardy Opens Fight to Resist Death Penalty," Jan. 2, 1948.

The Sacramento Bee (Calif.), "Lois Hardy's Fate Rests in Hands of Nevada City Jury," Dec. 18, 1947.

The Sacramento Bee (Calif.), "Lois Hardy Says She is Glad Jury Saved Mate's Life," Jan. 31, 1948.

The Sacramento Bee (Calif.), "Lois Hardy Tells Jury She Does Not Remember Killing," Dec. 15, 1947.

The Sacramento Bee (Calif.), "Lois Hardy Will Hear Date for Second Trial," Jan. 6, 1949.

The Sacramento Bee (Calif.), "Lois Hunt Hardy is Sentenced to Die For Slaying," Jan. 8, 1948.

The Sacramento Bee (Calif.), "Lure Slayers are Held to Answer Murder Charge," Aug. 7, 1947.

The Sacramento Bee (Calif.), "Lure Slayers Enter Not Guilty Pleas," Sept. 15, 1947.

The Sacramento Bee (Calif.), "Miscarriage of Justice," Feb. 4, 1949.

The Sacramento Bee (Calif.), "New Confession is Admitted in Trial of Hardy," Jan. 23, 1948.

The Sacramento Bee (Calif.), "Possibility of Delay Appears in Lois Hardy Trial," Jan. 26, 1949.

The Sacramento Bee (Calif.), "Presentation of Evidence Begins in Hardy Trial," Jan. 25, 1949.

The Sacramento Bee (Calif.), "Prosecution Seeks to Establish Sex Lure Slaying," Jan. 27, 1949.

The Sacramento Bee (Calif.), "Second Trial of Lois Hardy Will Begin on Monday," Jan. 22, 1949.

The Sacramento Bee (Calif.), "Sheriff Explains Delay in Leaving to Return Hardy," Dec. 6, 1957.

The Sacramento Bee (Calif.), "State Indirectly Asks Death for Joseph L. Hardy," Jan. 26, 1948.

The Sacramento Bee (Calif.), "State Prepares to Open Way for Hardy Confession," Jan. 21, 1948.

The Sacramento Bee (Calif.), "State Rests Case in Murder Trial of Joseph Hardy," Jan. 24, 1948.

The Sacramento Bee (Calif.), "Surprise Witness Links Lois to 'Lure Slaying,' Dec. 11, 1947.

The Sacramento Bee (Calif.), "Trial is Opened for Woman 'Lure' in Murder Case," Dec. 8, 1957.

The Sacramento Bee (Calif.), "Truckee Hearing is Held for 'Kiss of Death' Slayers," Aug. 6, 1947.

The Sacramento Bee (Calif.), "Truckee Matron's Story Links Lois Hardy to 'Lure' Slaying," Dec. 12, 1947.

The Sacramento Bee (Calif.), "Will is Written," Aug. 6, 1947.

The Union (Calif.), "Accused Woman Claims She Doesn't Remember Anything About Death," Dec. 15, 1947.

The Union (Calif.), "Court Admits Testimony of Dolley," Jan. 28,

1949.

The Union (Calif.), "Dolley Tells About Finding McLain's Body," Jan. 26, 1949.

The Union (Calif.), "Hardy Case to Go to Jury Tomorrow," Dec. 17, 1947.

The Union (Calif.), "Hardy Confession Admitted," Jan. 22, 1948.

The Union (Calif.), "Hardy Loses Fight Against Shell Evidence," Jan. 21, 1949.

The Union (Calif.), "Hardy Sentence to Life to be Fixed Tuesday," Jan. 28, 1948.

The Union (Calif.), "Hardy Trial Nears Finale," Feb. 1, 1949.

The Union (Calif.), "Judge Admits Parts of Hardy's Life Story," Jan. 23, 1948.

The Union (Calif.), "Jury Considering Hardy Case," Jan. 27, 1948.

The Union (Calif.), "Jury Finally Picked to Hear Jury Trial," Jan. 20, 1948.

The Union (Calif.), "Jury Says Lois is Innocent," Feb. 2, 1949.

The Union (Calif.), "Lois Hardy's Counsel Asks for New Trial," Dec. 19, 1948.

The Union (Calif.), "Officers Arrest," Jan. 27, 1949.

The Union (Calif.), "Selection of Jury Looks Like Long Drawn Out Affair," Jan. 19, 1948.

The Union (Calif.), "State Rests Case in Hardy Trial," Jan. 29, 1949.

The Union (Calif.), "Woman on Trial Tells of Meeting With 'Joey,'"

THE ENDS

Dec. 16, 1947.

U.S. Census Records, 1880, 1920, 1930, 1940.

U.S. City Directories, 1822-1995.

U.S. Public Records, 1970-2009.

U.S. Vital Records.

U.S. World War II Army Enlistment Records, 1938-1946.

U.S. World War II Draft Cards Young Men, 1940-1947.

INDEX

A

133

THE ENDS

140

ABOUT THE AUTHOR

Doresa Banning has an unwavering passion for writing, which led to her freelance career of crafting articles and other content for publications and businesses.

The thrill of unearthing and resuscitating buried information in story form drove her to pursue projects of her own, like *The Ends* and *It Really Happened!* The latter is Doresa's gambling history blog that showcases wild but true tales of casinos, celebrities, crime, corruption and much more.

Her book, *A Bold Gamble at Lake Tahoe: Crime and Corruption in a Casino's Evolution*, features Mobsters, lawsuits, celebrities, money woes, a stolen highway and much more. It chronicles the fascinating, rocky, 15-year development, from idea to stability, of a Northern Nevada hotel-casino that still operates today — the Hyatt Regency Lake Tahoe Resort.

The book is available in paperback and EPUB on Doresa's website and in paperback and Kindle on Amazon.

Though writing since kindergarten, the author truly learned and honed her craft at the University of California, San Diego (B.A. in writing and literature) and the University of Nevada, Reno (M.A. in journalism).

In her limited spare time, she loves to read, jog, solve crossword puzzles (in pencil), root for the Chargers, watch crime shows and crochet.

For more about Doresa, visit doresabanning.com. Feel free to connect with her there, at db@doresabanning.com or on Facebook, Twitter, LinkedIn or Instagram.

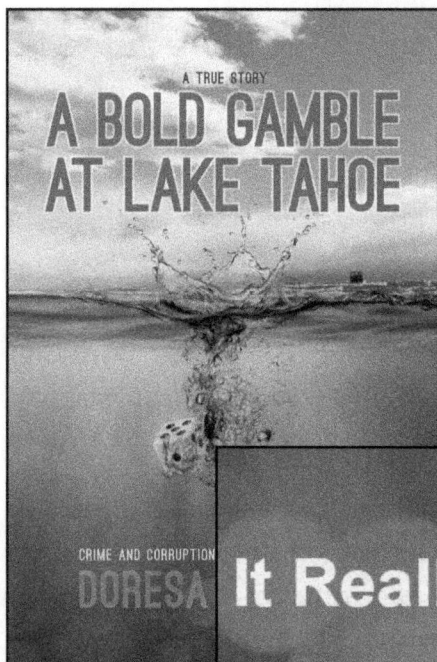

A TRUE STORY

A BOLD GAMBLE AT LAKE TAHOE

CRIME AND CORRUPTION

DORESA

It Really Happened!

Gambling History Blog

www.ingramcontent.com/pod-product-compliance
Lightning Source LLC
Chambersburg PA
CBHW021155020426
42331CB00003B/69